Praise for *The Epic Quest for Jesus*

This book is real. Full of terribly ~~~ ~ple just like me. For those of us v ~ ow eye opening to see Jesus at v  ted Him to be. The most impr witness the presence of God Jesus. In this book we see the g ... see what it means to be the beacon on the hill for others. Jesus is the beacon, not us. He is the light that shines through those who have faith to those who need Him. What Jimmy does is show us how to open our hearts and minds to Jesus. To trust the Lord with all things. When we do this the Holy Spirit has the opportunity to work miracles.

John M. Hetrick III, friend & brother-in-Christ

Jimmy's journey is an example of child-like faith and a display of Abraham-like obedience. As you read this book, you will be amazed and inspired seeing God work in his life and the lives he touched along the way. All to the glory of God!

Jim Sollenberger, mentor, friend, King Street Church

The Epic Quest for Jesus is the compelling witness of a once broken man, renewed by God, and used by Him to deliver the Good News of Christ from the back of a Harley. Every page demonstrates the power of the living God to mold and use Jimmy to transform the lives of people he encountered on his 20,464-mile journey across the US. Reading this inspiring work will give you a whole new perspective on answering the question, "Whom shall I send?"

Fred Ailes, Author, *The Bible and the Badge Devotional*

Jimmy's journey embodies the fact that there are no "chance" encounters and that if you are open and available, God's blessings will flow to you and through you. What I found extraordinary was how God was answering him in "real time." When we can eliminate the noise and distractions, as he was able to do, Jesus is patiently waiting and has been there the whole time. Jimmy's journey is living proof!

Raymond P. Cullen, mentor, friend, King Street Church

A number of years ago, I met Jimmy Rice in what I thought to be a chance meeting. I received a call that a guy who lived near me needed a ride to church. That guy was Jimmy. I got to know his story one ride at a time. Soon, I realized that meeting him was not by chance, but truly a blessing from God. You can ride along with Jim in *The Epic Quest for Jesus* as he hops on his Harley and canvasses the four corners of the United States to spread the Gospel in *his* quest for Jesus.

Rick Alexander, Operations Manager, Alpha Media

I've been impacted from the first time I read this incredible story. I challenge you to get on Jimmy's bike and take the ride of your life through this journey and see if you can rectify any of these almost-to-good-to-be-true 'coincidences' as anything other than the very hand of God.

Joanna Sanders, editor, author, friend

The Epic Quest for Jesus

Divine Encounters on My Four-Corners Ride

The Epic Quest for Jesus

James Rice

with Robert Jones

Copyright

James Rice, St. Thomas, Pennsylvania

Cover Design, Editing, Formatting: Joanna Sanders LLC
www.colossians46.com

Photo credits: James Rice

ISBN: 979-8-9863460-9-0 Paperback

ISBN: 979-8-9863460-8-3 eBook

To Heavyn, my precious daughter:

You are the best thing that has ever happened to me in this life, besides salvation. I will never forget the day you gave your life to Jesus. You made me the proudest daddy in the world. I know the "world" looks good to you right now, but I know you belong to Jesus. And one of these days He will bring you back to Himself and use your journey to glorify Him. He lives in your heart and I see Him live through you in the way that you take care of your siblings and other children. I am so proud of you and your caring heart. I love you, always and forever!

To Jason, my brother:

I miss you more than words can describe. The time we spent together on this earth meant the world to me. When you went home to be with Jesus, it broke my heart. But even from heaven you've helped me. I have peace knowing where you are and Who you're with. You are a true brother and I cannot wait to be reunited in heaven. DBF. I love you Brother!

To Jordan and Bryston:

My boys, I am honored to be your "Uncle" Jimmy. I have truly enjoyed watching you two grow into fine young men. Your dad is proud of you, I'm sure. As long as I'm alive you will always have an uncle that you can depend on to be there for you. I love you guys!

To my landlords, Don and Teresa:

I am very thankful for all that you guys have done for me over the years. You have truly been the hands and feet of Jesus. This journey would not have been possible without you. I'm blessed to have you two in my life. I love you guys!

Contents

FOREWORD

I've never been good at math, so my educated guess is that I've known Jimmy for about twelve years. I remember hearing him speak at the funeral of his best friend, Jason. Sometime later I heard his testimony at a men's event where I was the worship leader. I believe that this is where I first got to know him. Jimmy's story stuck with me. It was different, authentic, and real. His message resonated with those in attendance.

As time went on, we became friends, through Sunday School and church. Jimmy's background is different than mine. He grew up in the country, I grew up next to the city of Philadelphia. Jimmy is an avid motorcyclist, I prefer bicycles. Jimmy likes snakes, I have two cats. We are very different but I know a few things about him. First, God has totally changed his life, from a path of rebellion and destruction, to a heart of love and service. Second, based on his story, he can relate to people that others cannot because he has "been there and done that." I also know that his life's passion is to love and serve both God and people. In spite of our varied backgrounds and interests, we share this same passion and are brothers in Christ as a result.

A number of years ago, when my wife first heard Jimmy's story in Sunday School, she said to me, "Honey, someone should write a book about Jimmy, it could help a lot of people. Maybe that person is you." I gave a lengthy response to my wife, "Ah, no!" At that point, I had never written a book and had no idea of the process or where one would even start.

Fast forward to 2020 when Jimmy embarked on his journey to the four corners of the United States. My wife again said, "Maybe someone should write a book about Jimmy's story and journey." I agreed that "someone" should do this but I knew that the someone wasn't me. I was sure that I did not have the skills and I firmly believed that there were many more-qualified people to take on such a project. Granted, I also never dreamed that I would ever write one book, let alone two, about stories in my own life. Now looking back, I reflect that writing books was one of the hardest things I'd ever done. It was only through God's wisdom, strength, and an amazing writing coach/editor that I was able to pull it off. To even consider writing a book for someone else's story? Impossible! But with Him, all things are possible. Sometimes it takes me awhile to get on board with God's plans. When will I ever learn?

In October of 2021, I was in the midst of my quiet time when I heard that voice in my spirit: "Bob, you need to help Jimmy write a book." I quickly dismissed the thought. This can't be from God. He knows that I don't have it in me to take on such a task. But as the days passed, I kept hearing the same thing. Okay, I know the verse that says that we are to "test the spirits to see whether they are from God" (1 John 4:1), so I decided to contact Jimmy and ask him out to lunch. Surely if God was speaking to me, He'll tell Jimmy the same thing. Secretly I believed (and hoped) that he would not be interested in a book but more in getting back on the road.

At that lunch date I learned that Jimmy had been praying that the Lord would send someone to help him get his story out. He told me that I was the answer to his prayers. That wasn't what I expected to hear. I explained, "Jimmy, I don't think I have the skills to do this and there are a number of more-qualified people in the church who might possibly help with this." Jimmy wasn't deterred so I asked him to pray about it further. I offered to contact my editor, Joanna, and get her opinion about the idea. Surely, she would say something like, "Well, it's a great idea Bob but..." Several days later, Jimmy, Joanna, and I met on a video call. Jimmy gave the cliff-notes version of his journey and Joanna, obviously moved by his story, said, "Bob, we have to help Jimmy write this book." So here we are!

I am actually writing this Foreword one day after my initial interview with Jimmy for this book. I don't know what the final version will look like but I know that God is in this. It's cliché but this has confirmed for me once again that God does not always call the qualified, but He certainly qualifies the called. For reasons beyond my understanding, God has prepared me for such a time, (and task) as this. Now I need to get out of the way and allow you to see the awesomeness of God through Jimmy's life and journey.

I pray that I would do justice to Jimmy's story. Above all, I pray that the Lord Jesus Christ would be honored and glorified through the amazing story of what He has done in Jimmy's life.

Robert Jones
Author of *Average Man, Almighty Companion* and *Family Love Letters*

INTRODUCTION

I rode 20,464 miles on my Harley.

A trip that lasted six months and two days, and spanned more than 29 states.

But now, almost a year later, looking around at the four walls of my house, I was getting restless.

My dream journey began on October 10, 2020, which also happened to be my daughter's 17th birthday. I still couldn't believe that God called and allowed me to take that incredible journey, as well as several subsequent smaller trips. God had spoken to me continually in so many ways and I was ready again for my next adventure. "Lord, I am ready to ride again. Where do you want me to go?" Like the prophet Isaiah, I said, "Here am I Lord, send me." But for some reason God seemed to be silent. All I kept hearing in my spirit was, "Be still, Jimmy."

"But you know my heart, Lord. I want to tell people about You. I want to help the homeless and those who are down and out. I have a dream of starting a biker ministry, maybe even a church." I had argued with God when He first called me to go, but now, I was "all in." "Lord, where do You want to send me now?" The still small voice repeated, "Be still Jimmy, and know that I am God."

I didn't understand but I obeyed. I continue to learn that God honors obedience. He certainly did on my journey. So, as hard as it was for me, I decided that I would be still. One thing I had been praying about was for a means to tell my story and launch whatever ministry God had for me. A number of trusted friends had been telling me that I needed to write a book to capture my testimony and journey. Above all, I wanted my life to bring glory to Him, so if a book could honor God, I would continue to pray about it.

People who know me know that I am transparent. What you see is what you get. So, I admit that I am not much of a reader or a writer. I knew that if God was calling me to tell my story, especially in a book format, I would need help. But who? All I could do was be still and continue to pray. "Lord, if it's Your will, please send someone to help me write a book, not for me, but to tell everyone what You've done in my life."

Another thing I learned on my journey, (something I've known for a while, but have seen proven over and over in the past year), is that God is interested in every detail of our lives. He answers our prayers! That was the case once more. His answer came through an unexpected text from my friend, Bob. As soon as we sat down at lunch and Bob explained the thoughts he was having, I knew that this was an answer to my prayers. I could tell that Bob wasn't too sure that he wanted to do this, nor that he even could. But I knew that this was God's will. I knew that God would enable us to bring this book to completion for His glory. And He confirmed it through a number of other people.

I'd like to invite you to come along on my journey and experience how awesome God is. That's the reason for this book. You see, I believe that you can't look at my journey and not see God all through it. The evidence of His love and provision, the lives He touched along the way (including mine), the miracles He performed. It's beyond human understanding. I also want to give you hope.

I wish that I could share every story and divine encounter from my journey but they would fill several books and likely take years to compile. Instead, I had to make some hard decisions as to which stories to include in the book. I want to extend my sincerest gratitude and love to those who prayed for me, provided financially, housed and fed me, supported me, and just plain loved me. To those I met along the way, (many of whom are friends now and check in on me regularly), thank you from the bottom of my heart. If space allowed it, I would mention each of you by name. I will never forget your kindness.

My friends, Jesus Christ has totally transformed my life, from a sinner who ran from Him, to an undeserving child of God. Being a Christian is not about being perfect, because none of us can be. It's about total dependence upon

God and relying on the blood of Jesus to be righteous before Him. It has nothing to do with my good works but everything to do with what Jesus Christ did 2000 years ago, by dying on a cruel cross for my sins. He offers that same gift to you and my prayer is that you will ask Jesus to forgive you of your sins and receive that amazing gift! Time is short and none of us are guaranteed tomorrow. The message is urgent; which is why my passion is to tell everyone I meet about Jesus and what He has done for me. No matter who you are, no matter your past, whether you're rich or poor, whatever your circumstances, God can save you and transform your life. If He did that for me, He is more than able to do that for you. Know that our souls will live for eternity in one of two places: Heaven or Hell. Choose wisely my friends.

God loves you and has a plan for your life. I pray that you will seek Him while there is still time, and receive all that He has in store for you. Life will not be perfect but you will have joy beyond what you can imagine. He wants to take you places you've never been, to be encouraged, and to encourage others.

I invite you now to join me on the ride of a lifetime. I can't wait for you to experience the places I saw, the people I met, and most of all the awesome God who sustained me and made it all possible!

Your friend and brother,

Jimmy (a.k.a. "Billboard")

ABOUT MY ROAD NAME, "BILLBOARD"

I included my road name of "Billboard" because many on my journey only know me by that name. My friend and sister in Christ, Amy, from the Broken Chains Biker Church (you'll read about her in Chapter 5) gave me the name on December 2, 2020 when I was in New Mexico visiting my friend Brian. She sent me a text message which read, "Your road name is "Billboard" because you are a walking, talking billboard for the Broken Chains Biker Church and the Lord Jesus Christ, as you travel the country with your hoodie on, telling people about Jesus."

Ironically, I did not want to use that name because it wasn't "biker-enough" for me. But a few days after Amy sent the message, I pulled out my earbuds and noticed the word "Billboard" on the side of one of the earbuds. I took this as a sign from God and have used the name ever since.

BEFORE THE EPIC QUEST

Before we get into my journey to the four corners of our beautiful country, I would like to tell you how I got here. That story is a miracle in itself!

I was born and raised in South Central Pennsylvania. I have a brother and two half-brothers, one of whom sadly died from a drug overdose. I have been married three times and have a precious teenage daughter, Heavyn, who I love with all of my heart.

I was not raised in a Christian home and did not have a storybook childhood. Dad and Mom were into alcohol and drugs. Dad left home when I was only five years old. As a result, we moved around a lot and there was no real stability in my life. All praise to God, Mom and Dad are no longer who they were back then.

Mom sent me to church, but did not attend herself. Nothing I was taught in church stuck with me. God was not a part of my life at all. In fact, I cursed God and wanted nothing to do with Him. I couldn't understand how He could allow all of these bad things to happen to my family. My grandfather (Pappy Rice), my uncle Don, and uncle Jerry were my mentors and they sincerely invested in my life, for which I am grateful. But they could not be there all the time like a dad should be. I know that, ultimately, I am responsible for the things I've done in my life but my upbringing did not start me out on the right foot.

Before long, my pent-up anger revealed itself in violent ways. In fourth grade, I threw a chair at a teacher. This was one of many examples of my rebellion. In my teens, I got involved with alcohol and drugs. As I think about it now, I realize that I was looking for attention from my dad. The more I got into trouble, the more attention I got. This was not the attention I was looking for, but, in my mind, it was better than nothing.

When I was about seventeen years old, I got involved with the Ku Klux Klan (KKK) and joined the organization within a year. Growing up where I did, friends and I pretended to be in the KKK. I became a "Nighthawk," which is the head of security, and remained in that position until I left. Even then, in my rebellion, I know that God was working in my life; He placed the realization on my heart that I needed to leave that hateful organization.

Eventually my rebellion and lifestyle caught up with me. Alcohol played a huge part in my sinful behavior and the consequences I would face. Between the drinking, drugs, and unhealthy relationships with women, I was out of control and often hitting rock bottom. I was in such mental pain and I cared about no one, including myself.

Over the years, I would be in and out of jail six times, mostly for Driving Under the Influence (DUI) and various violations.

I would experience the hefty consequences of my behavior, and then go on to try to live better, for a while. But it was a constant struggle. In 2001, my best friend, "Little Brad" committed suicide, and I was devastated. The pain was overwhelming and I once again reverted to a destructive lifestyle. I ended up back in jail, but was eventually released under house arrest and moved in with my grandmother.

I had no interest in God or church, but my grandmother tricked me into going to church; she offered several arguments about why I should go to church. She told me that going to church would allow me to get out of the house and would look good to my probation officer. I wasn't convinced though, until she told me that there were a few single ladies at her church. I didn't tell her, but meeting girls was the best reason to go, so I agreed!

From the first time I went, the pastor's messages spoke to me, so much so, that I started going to church regularly. God spoke to me through the messages, and I felt like He was speaking directly to me, like He knew all about my life! One Sunday, there was an altar call and I couldn't hold back any longer; I stood up to go forward. The people in the congregation knew all about my life and my past, so there were audible gasps when they saw me stand up!

I didn't care what anyone thought, I went forward to the altar, dropped to my knees and prayed. Gradually I could feel hands on my shoulders as people came forward to pray over me. I cried tears of joy and surrendered all to the Lord. I can't describe the weight that was lifted off of my shoulders. In spite of who I was and all I'd done, Jesus paid it all for me. All I could do was surrender to Jesus and allow Him to direct my life. When I stood to return to my seat, I saw an awesome sight: most of the church had come forward to pray over me. And I know that many had been praying for my salvation and their prayers were answered on that beautiful Sunday.

However, years later, even as a saved Christian man, I had backslidden tremendously. With stress and pressure, I found myself reverting to the old remedies of the past; drinking and drugs. While I was solely responsible for my own choices, I had no accountability partners or consistent mentors to help me grow in my Christian walk. I realize now how important that might have been for me. As the result of my third DUI and an assault charge, I was sentenced to state prison and spent three years and three months there.

Whenever I tell my story I include the statement, "Going to prison saved my life." It was actually Jesus who saved my life while I was incarcerated. Had I not gone to prison and then rededicated my life to Him there, I am convinced that I would not be here today.

For the first nine months back in prison, I contemplated and prepared to end my life. One night, I carefully tied my bed sheets together, planning to hang myself. I just couldn't take it anymore. Even though I had cursed God and rejected Him, I cried out in desperation. "If You're real, please help me." God, in His love and mercy, in spite of who I was, and what I had done, spoke to me that night. He convinced me that my life had meaning and worth, and that my precious daughter needed me. He also made it clear that I needed help and couldn't do this by myself. I untied the sheet and made the bed. The next morning, I waited to see what would happen next.

Miraculously, God sent Kelvin to me. I had met Kelvin at an Alcoholics Anonymous (AA) meeting on the "block," the common area of the prison where inmates would congregate. I shared my past with him, including my experience with the KKK. Kelvin is a black man but never judged me for my past, he just loved me. Kelvin led me back to the Lord and encouraged me to attend church in prison. Because of him, I became a lead usher in the prison church which prepared me to usher later on when I was released from prison. Kelvin and I are brothers in Christ and we still keep in touch and encourage each other to this day. God sent this man into my life to save it!

As I look back at my prison experience, I am reminded that a large percentage of incarcerated men did not have a father growing up. Dads, we need to do better and take responsibility. Again, I'm responsible for the things

I've done but I wonder if things would have been different if my father had been more involved with me.

JASON

I would not be the man I am today without my best friend, Jason. We met around the year 2000, riding four-wheelers. For some reason, we just clicked and became inseparable. We did everything together and I truly love that man. We are brothers. Notice that I refer to Jason in the present tense because he is alive; he is in heaven, waiting for me with Jesus. When I was released from prison in 2009 it was Jason who took me in, gave me a place to live and a fresh start.

When Jason and I would text each other, the messages were always short:

How are you doing?

I'm fine.

See you tonight.

On April 15, 2011, Jason sent me this unusually long text:

Hey, I just wanted to tell you how proud I am of you. What your walk has been is tremendous from where you've been. I'm so proud to call you my brother. Just keep in mind to thank our God for your struggles and the past you once had because if it wasn't for them, you wouldn't be the man you are today. I can tell that God is smiling down on you, for the man He has created has found His grace and forgiveness. Praise God for our stumbles each day, for it brings us closer to Him with each prayer and devotional experience. I love you. You know I'm here each and every day if any of you need me.

Peace,

Your brother, Jason

About two hours after I received the above text from Jason, he was gone. I remember being on my way home from work when I received a call from one of my pastors. He had some news for me but would not tell me until I was safe in my driveway. I insisted that I wanted to hear the message but the pastor would not budge. When I finally arrived at home, the pastor gave me the news: Jason had died in a motorcycle accident. I blacked out and an eerie, hollow sound pierced through my brain. I was devastated. After cleaning myself up from work I headed to the hospital where I said goodbye to my best friend, the one who I could always lean on. Looking back now, I know that Jason's message was prophetic, and somehow God was preparing me for what was to come that day. It hurt and still does but I am comforted by the fact that Jason is in the arms of His Father in heaven.

That same evening, I was scheduled to practice and do a sound check in church for a testimony I was to give on Sunday. As I passed by a local tavern, I made the decision to deaden my pain with alcohol; I was ready to get drunk and forget about the darkness of the day. But before I could go in, God spoke to me and I could hear Jason's voice and his words. Jason wanted me to go to church. His text said that he was proud of me and I knew I couldn't let him down. So, I went to church and on Sunday gave my testimony. The impact of Jason's life made my story that much more powerful.

Thankfully, there have been countless Christian men who have come beside me for encouragement and accountability. No one could replace Jason but God provides exactly what and who we need, and exactly when we need it. We all need someone to lean on and we can be the shoulder for someone else.

I keep a memorial place in my house which pays tribute to Jason's life. In addition to a large cross and pictures of Jason, me, and our kids, I have this framed poem Jason wrote prominently displayed on my wall. The poem is called "Second Chance" and I want to share it with you:

I feel this is my time, I don't want to be last in line

Every time we're together I get a chill I let it all into His will

I had to figure out; it's not always my way

That's all I can say.

Today is a new day, this is my chance. A feeling that makes you want to dance.

My eyes are open wide with you by my side.

There are days you need to lean on a brother

But we all need to look toward our Father

Angels heard my cries for help the day

You reached out to listen and say, it will be okay.

We are not all the same, No longer do you have to live in shame

Sometimes people do things we cannot explain

They can hurt us and cause us pain

But God has the hands to lay you down

He can comfort you and not let you drown

When we say goodbye to our past You get a Second Chance.

Peace, Jason

GOD PREPARES ME FOR SERVICE

Who knew that God would use my past experiences and passions to prepare me for the journey of a lifetime? As I write this book, I realize God was orchestrating several things in my life, in His perfect timing, to not only fulfill His plan, but to satisfy desires in my own heart.

God used my love for the outdoors as a foundation for what was to come. Hunting and fishing have always been a big part of my life and I love the mountains. I rode mini-bikes and go-carts as a kid and wore biker garb. My mantra when I was a kid was, "When I turn 18, I'm going to buy a Heritage Softail and ride it to Sturgis, South Dakota for the bike rally, not 'trailer it like a sissy.'" (This is not meant to be disrespectful, but is an expression used by hardcore bikers.) Well, I had to wait until the year 2012 to fulfill the dream of owning the Harley. Little did I know what God would call me to do with the bike. Also, my dream back then was to ride to Sturgis and hang out with the women and party. I had no idea that I would one day go to Sturgis to tell people about Jesus!

God also used my prison experience to prepare me for mission's work. When I left prison, I was willing to help in any way I could, so I started by setting up chairs for our church's contemporary worship service. Eventually the Lord opened up opportunities for me to become an usher and a Sunday School teacher. I already had experience as an usher from prison church! God also called me to speak at local churches, for men's and youth groups, where I've had the opportunity to tell my story and the radical transformation God has done in my life. Through all of this, He has given me a heart for the lost and those who cannot help themselves. Understand that this is not my doing, it is all His!

In 2015, I was asked to accompany several church members on a mission's trip to Haiti. Our church has a partnership with a ministry in Haiti and made several trips to erect a new church building in country. Jason's father was the head of the committee that organized the trip. When he asked me to go, I have to be honest, I had to pray about it. My past with the KKK came to mind and I wondered how that would sit in a country like Haiti. After a time of intense prayer, I was convinced I had to go. I knew that God could use my past, as He always has, for something good.

I have now made four trips to Haiti. I went there thinking that I would be a blessing to them. It turns out that they blessed me more, especially the precious children! I was moved to tears at how little the people have in Haiti. We take so much for granted; ample food, water, a bed to sleep in, even toilets. They have so little, yet so much joy. Their love for God and passion to worship should make us reexamine our lives here in America where we have so much.

Based on all that the Lord has taught and done for me, I have a passion for people and seek opportunities to help, even in the simplest ways. I had my own ministry where I would coordinate supplying needy people with basic necessities. If someone had a flat tire, I would fix it. If a family needed a bed, or washer, or dryer, I would canvass the community for a donation and even move the appliances and hook them up. There are so many out there who cannot help themselves for a variety of reasons. I have a God-given desire to help everyone I can.

Unfortunately, due to some health issues I can no longer do the physical work I would like to do. While this fact contributed to a state of depression, God used it as another building block to my journey. But before that happened, things were about to get rough. I was about to go through a storm which almost ended my life. And that's where my journey began ...

THE JOURNEY OF A LIFETIME

I have loved to work with my hands since I was a child. My father and my Pappy Rice were mechanics, and "Pap" taught me everything he knew about cars and many other skills. My Pap could fix anything!

When I left prison in 2009, I was on fire for Jesus. I had so many dreams that I was sure God would honor. Above all I wanted to work in the ministry field, perhaps with prisoners. But every door I tried to open was shut. Based on my criminal record and the fact that I had no college degree, no one would give me a chance. Very quickly, my "fire" became a smoldering log. But I was comforted by the words of Proverbs 16:9: "In their hearts humans plan their course, but the Lord establishes their steps."

After I left prison, I also reconnected with my high school crush. We dated on and off for a while. She was not a believer when we got together, but eventually made a confession of faith. She told me, "Jimmy, I want what you've got." She was baptized and volunteered to serve in church. Ultimately, we got married and for the first five years, things were great. She had a daughter who amazingly was friends with my daughter in school. They got along well and we became a family. It seemed like a marriage made in heaven.

In order to support myself and my family, I obtained a job as an auto mechanic at a local garage. This was not the path I wanted to take, but I trusted God that He could use me in whatever capacity He placed me. Between my marriage, job, church ministries, and serving others, life was good and I believed that I was right where I needed to be. Still, deep inside, I continued to have this desire to do something bigger for God.

In December of 2018, I suspected that my wife was having an affair. Something was "off" with her and I strongly sensed that something was wrong. In March of 2019, my suspicions were confirmed and I caught her together with another man. I confronted him at his home, and in my anger came close to doing something I would regret. Truly, God stopped me from hurting this man because I was in a rage. The situation was made worse by the fact that my first and second marriages ended in a similar manner; due to infidelity. Back then my anger got the best of me and I acted on it.

After things cooled down, I sensed God speaking to me. "Jimmy, do you want to save your marriage? I forgave you; you must forgive your wife." As difficult as this was, I forgave her 30 minutes later. My wife seemed to be repentant and I praised God that things seemed to be getting back to where they were. This did not last long, unfortunately.

In October of 2019, my wife asked me to move out of the house. She said, "Find somewhere to live for the rest of the week." I packed a small bag and spent the next week sleeping in the back of the garage where I worked. I inflated an air mattress each night and deflated it the next morning. The back room had basic provisions such as a sink, toilet, and shower. I lived on fast food while I pondered what the future might hold.

At the end of the week, my wife asked my daughter and I to leave for good. This was a sad moment, not only for my marriage, but for Heavyn also. I continued to work on the marriage after securing living quarters for my daughter and me. At times, it appeared that my wife was open to reconciliation and I praised God. But on December 21, 2020, my wife divorced me.

In July of 2020, my daughter moved out. In my mind, I raised her with morals and taught her right from wrong. She made a confession of faith at nine years old. Unfortunately, as was the case in my own younger years, the world got ahold of my precious daughter. I pray continually for her return to the Lord. With the things she was into, I would not allow her to continue that behavior in my home. Sadly, she moved out of my house and in with her mother who does not adhere to the boundaries that I keep. This just added to the pain I felt from the ending of my marriage.

While all of this was going on, I was experiencing severe back pain, to the point where I could hardly walk. This excruciating pain made it difficult and often impossible to perform my job as an auto mechanic. I was taking heavy medication to manage the pain. But I was sinking fast. This was the proverbial straw that broke the camel's back.

On September 17, 2020 I truly hit rock bottom. I could no longer take the physical and emotional pain. My wife and daughter had left, and I could hardly walk. It hurt so badly and I couldn't take it anymore. I sat in the bathroom at work, somewhere where I could be alone, and cried. I decided that I would drive to my family cabin that night, back in the woods to my hunting blind, and use my 444 Marlin rifle to put a bullet in my head. I was finished.

Just before I stood up to walk out of the bathroom, God spoke to me. "Jimmy, you can't let Satan destroy what I've done in your life." I was reminded that He had brought me through years of alcohol and drug abuse (praise the Lord I now have over 15 years of sobriety). He also rescued me from the KKK, saved my life many times, and brought me through prison, and had used me on mission's trips. Above all, He shed His blood on the cross and saved my soul from an eternity in hell.

In my mind, I knew all of that, but I couldn't take how I was feeling. I swore, hollered, cried, and argued with God. "Lord, what do you want me to do?" God gently spoke to me and asked, "Jimmy what could you do every day that would make you happy and bring you joy?" I responded, "That's easy, I want to tell people about You and what

You've done in my life. That's all I've ever wanted to do since I've gotten out of prison, but no one will give me a chance!" The Lord wasn't finished as He followed up, "What else do you love to do?" I said, "You already know; I've ushered, taught Sunday School, gone on mission's trips to Haiti, had my own ministry to help out the less fortunate, I love people and serving You."

The conversation didn't end there. "Jimmy, what do you do for you when you're having a bad day. What brings you joy?" I had an easy answer for that one too. "I jump on my Harley and ride up into the mountains, get alone and talk with You, and just enjoy the beauty of Your Creation."

What came next excited me ... at first. I felt God saying, "Jimmy, get on your bike and go tell people about Me and what I've done in your life." I can do that, I thought. There are lots of people in my community and surrounding areas here in Pennsylvania. But what came next was unexpected. "No, Jimmy, your first stop is Bangor, Maine." Wait, what?! This made no sense at all. It was almost October, and fall weather was already settling in Pennsylvania. I knew that it was going to be much colder in Maine. This is crazy! All I could sense from God was the simple phrase, "I'll take care of you."

While I was arguing with God in the little bathroom at my workplace, He reminded me of a hunting trip Jason and I were supposed to take back in the mid-2000s. Guess where we had planned to go? Bangor, Maine. Jason did get to go on that trip, but I had gotten into some trouble at the time and didn't have the money to go. Now it seemed like

27

this was God's way for me to take the trip with Jason after all. Although my best friend was no longer with me, I had such a peace about the destination God was calling me to. I thought about Jason a lot on the way to Maine and the entire time I was there.

Not satisfied though with the limited information I had, I asked, "Then what, Lord, what comes after Maine?" This next response was more than I could take. "Hit the other three corners of the U.S., Jimmy." I argued with God again: "Lord, how can I possibly do that? Do you expect me to quit my job and leave my house empty? How will I live, where will I get the money? What about gas for my bike, and food? What if my bike breaks down, how will I pay for repairs?" Then I thought about my excruciating back pain. "And how will I spend that much time on my bike? One of the reasons I'm sitting here is that I am in unbearable pain!"

Then the Lord quoted a passage which appears in Matthew and Luke. What I heard was, "Jimmy I care for the sparrows and how much more important are you?" I didn't want to hear Scripture, so I was obstinate and continued to argue with God. I've learned something through the many trials, valleys, and mountaintops where God has walked with me: If it's His will, He will gently and sometimes not-so-gently lead you in that direction. I am so grateful that He has been patient and never given up on me. "Jimmy, you've been telling me for years that you wanted Me to use you, now I'm asking you to go and you don't want to." I said, "It's not that I don't want to go but it's impossible." He gently reminded me: "Remember that all things are possible with

Me, son." There was Scripture again, but my heart had softened. I finally stood up, left the bathroom, and went back to work. God had saved my life once more.

For the rest of the day at work, I wrestled with God in my mind. I could feel Him working in my life and His Spirit carried me through the remainder of the day in such a powerful way.

I finished the day at work and went home and took a shower. As I looked over at my gun cabinet, I audibly said, "Not today, Satan." I was so worn out mentally and physically that I couldn't function. I was sick to my stomach and couldn't eat. I went to bed around seven that evening but sleep did not come easily. I still had questions and wrestled with God some more. This whole idea just didn't make sense. At some point I fell asleep.

I woke up to the sound of my alarm clock at 6:00a.m. on Friday morning. I didn't understand it but I had a peace that I can't describe. I looked in the mirror and had a smile on my face. I prayed, "Lord, Your Word says that You cannot lie, it's impossible. So, I know that You have never lied to me. If You are telling me to go, I'll go."

I got dressed and went to work as I usually did on Fridays. At lunchtime I took my two bosses aside and gave my two-week notice. They asked me where I was going and what I would be doing, so I told them: "I'm going to ride my Harley to the four-corners of this country and tell everyone I meet about Jesus!" As excited as I was, the look on their faces told me that they thought I was out of my mind. My last two weeks at the shop were rough.

That same Friday night I called my landlords and told them that we needed to have a conversation. We planned to meet on the following Friday night. During the week I asked God to help me pack my bike. I needed His wisdom to determine what I would need to take on the trip. I also thoroughly checked over my bike to ensure that it was ready for this long trip. I packed the things I would need for camping, including a tent, portable heater, and lantern. Can you guess how many times I unpacked and set up my tent on the journey? Zero. Not once. You'll understand why once we get to the end of my story.

That Friday I had the meeting with my landlords. I've alluded to this before but I like to "keep it real," so I told them the story of how I was going to put a bullet in my head but God spoke to me about my impending journey to the four corners of the U.S. I further explained that I had quit my job and had just enough money to pay the rent for the current month. I asked if it would be okay if the house remained empty during my journey. I told my landlords that if I was gone for a month, I would send them a check because God said He would supply all my needs.

Confirmation came from my landlord, Teresa, who said this: "Jimmy, if you're going to ride north to Maine in October to tell people about Jesus, your rent is paid whether you're gone for two months or two years." I cried like a little baby, again, amazed at the goodness of God.

Words cannot describe all that my landlords did and the time they invested in me. While I was away, they would retrieve my mail and go over my bills and correspondence once each week with me. They ran the water, flushed the toilets, and kept the house in order. They did so many other things which allowed me to pursue what God called me to do on my journey. I am eternally grateful.

The day before I planned to leave on my journey, I headed towards Jordan and Bryston's place to say goodbye. Jordan and Bryston are Jason's children and I love them dearly. They call me "Uncle Jimmy." I had not driven very far when my cell phone rang. It was my daughter, Heavyn, who wanted to see me. I hadn't seen her in months so I quickly turned around and drove back to my house where she was waiting for me. This call brought joy to me and I considered it a test from the Lord. In my conversations with the Lord, I had determined that the only reason I would not go on this journey was if Heavyn came home. I was convinced that the Lord was testing me, reminding me of the time when He tested Abraham with his son, Isaac. I surmised that like Abraham, I had "passed" the test, since I was willing to go. Now I wondered if the Lord was returning my daughter to me because of my obedience.

When I got to the house, Heavyn was waiting in her vehicle. I hugged her and we talked and cried. We took a picture together and I thought that she was coming home. The reality is, she had only come to see me off before I left on my journey. Her birthday was the very next day, the day I planned to leave. I wanted to spend the next day with her but she had other plans. I was crushed. "Lord, why would you do this, I don't understand?" I sensed the Lord telling me that it was Satan, the enemy of our souls, who was trying to impede my journey. After Heavyn left, I went and said goodbye to Jason's boys.

I went to bed on Friday night and left the house at 6:30 Saturday morning, October 10, 2020.

My Thursday men's group wanted to see me off before I left, so we met at a local restaurant. While these are my close brothers in Christ, I think that they secretly thought that my journey was a crazy idea. I understood! From a human perspective it didn't make much sense. But the Lord had saved my life and aligned too many things for this to be a "coincidence," so I was going in faith.

My dear brothers treated me to breakfast. We talked, shared the Scriptures, and prayed. When breakfast was finished, we all walked outside and the men prayed over me and my bike. I hugged each one and we shook hands. The last brother to shake my hand transferred some money to me. "This is just the start, brother," he said. I cried when I left and even more as I made my ride through Pennsylvania. Actually, I shed more tears on this trip than I ever have in my life.

A Map of My Journey

THE FIRST CORNER

"MAINE" EVENTS

After stopping for gas, not too far from home, I was on my way. My goal was to make it to Bangor as quickly as possible, stopping only for bathroom breaks and gas. Whenever I visited a convenience store on one of my stops, I would also grab a snack. This was the way I rolled for the entire journey unless the Lord had other plans, which of course, He often did. Many times, along the way, my ride was "interrupted" and I spent time talking to people at gas stations/convenience stores. Since I continually asked the Lord for opportunities to talk about Him, I considered these chance meetings as "divine encounters."

My first divine encounter happened in New York state that afternoon with a dear woman named "Kate." I had stopped at a gas station and put $10 worth of fuel into my Harley. I went inside the store to use the facilities and when I came out noticed Kate standing by my bike.

As I walked to my bike, she called to me and said, "That's a beautiful bike and you have so much stuff on it. What are you doing?" I told her my story, that God had sent me on a journey to the four corners of the country to tell people about Him. I explained that I was on my way to the first corner, Maine.

Kate was floored! "Here, I want to help you," she said, and she handed me some cash which happened to be twice as much as I had just paid to fill up my tank. Not only was God answering my prayers to bring people to me, but He provided 100% more than I just spent! I was witnessing His love and abundant care for me in real time!

"Are you documenting your trip?" she asked. I told Kate that I was posting a journal of my journey on Facebook at the end of each day. She was not on Facebook so asked for my phone number to keep track of my progress. Within a month, Kate had signed up for Facebook and sent me a friend request so that she could see more details of the trip. This random stranger, who is now a friend and sister, blessed me abundantly right out of the gate. I never would have met her had I not gone on this journey, and I now hear from her almost every day!

There are so many like Kate who encouraged, supported, and blessed me on the journey. To each one, starting with Kate, I always made this sincere offer: "If you ever get to Pennsylvania, you have a place to stay." Months later, after I returned from my journey, Kate showed up at my house on a surprise visit. She was the first of several people to take me up on that offer. On a side note: "Panhead Mike," a man I met on my second journey to Broken Chains

Biker Church, one of the last people I offered a place to stay, showed up at my house the day Kate left!

My heart was filled with joy as I left the gas station and got back on the road. I rode until dark and was still in New York state that evening. I prayed and asked God where I should stay. This was something I prayed every night on my journey when I was on the road and He always provided. I sensed God telling me to keep riding. Then it began raining and driving became difficult. I heard God say, "Go to the light," and at that moment, I saw the light of a building. I located a recessed doorway where my bike and I would be safe from the elements. That is where I slept that night.

When I woke up the next morning, the light of day revealed that I had spent the night at a church. Of all of the places God could have sent me, I was at a church! I did not encounter a single person, and to this day, I don't know if anyone else knew that I had been there. But God gave me what I needed at exactly the right time.

BANGOR, MAINE

It was day two of my journey and I was back on the road. The ride that day consisted of a lot of driving, stops for gas and bathrooms, and snacks. On my rides, I survived on a lot of quick meals. As a side note, I shed about sixty pounds by the end of my journey! My stops were always quick unless the Lord brought someone across my path who needed encouragement.

As part of my routine, I had been taking oxycontin three times a day for back pain. After I had taken my

39

morning dose that day, God spoke to me and said, "Quit taking the pills, you don't need them anymore." I thought, "I've been taking these for years, how is that going to work." I sensed Him saying, "Just stop, I'll take care of you." I questioned the Lord in my spirit but obeyed anyway. The blessing is that I have not taken the pills since then. God still never ceases to amaze me!

I arrived in Maine that evening but the light had faded and I was still an hour and a half from Bangor. I wanted to stop for the day. I had this strange dream where I had hit a moose and fear entered my mind. I prayed and sensed God's voice telling me to keep going, "I've got you, Jimmy." I rode almost two more hours in the dark and I was frozen. Maine was even colder than I had imagined and I did not have the right gear for the weather. My gloves and leather clothing were just not cutting it.

A bit of relief came when I saw the road sign for Bangor. However, I wondered what to do next when upon a closer look, I noticed the words, "Next 6 Exits." Now what do I do? Which exit do I take? The first? The sixth? I prayed and kept asking God which exit to take. I was so cold and just wanted to get off of the road.

When I came upon the second exit for Bangor, I sensed from the Lord that I needed to get off here. I came to a stop sign but it was decision time again. Do I go left or right? I felt God saying "right" so that's where I went.

Before too long I came upon a big white building on the left and God told me to pull into the parking lot. It turned out to be a church and I was encouraged that there were people in the parking lot. But as soon as I got close, they began to scatter, I can only assume out of fear. Now, I'm a big guy and may look intimidating to some, but this was a church! As people were walking away, I said in a loud voice, "I'm a Christian, I'm looking for help!" Some people came back and eventually the pastor came out to meet me. He listened to my story and I asked where I might be able to stay for the night. I stated that a shed, abandoned car, or any enclosed area would suffice. The pastor said, "We can't help you but there are hotels nearby. Can you be in my office at 10 tomorrow morning? I'd like to hear more of your story." I agreed and headed off to find a hotel.

I found what appeared to be a hotel but the doors were locked when I tried to enter. I saw people inside, so I knocked. A lady came to the door. I learned that this hotel had been converted to a homeless shelter. I asked the nice woman, Angela, if I could stay for the night. After all, technically, I was homeless. But bureaucracy prevented me from staying. She apologetically told me that I would need to fill out paperwork to formally apply to stay there. I was disappointed, but Angela directed me to a nearby hotel where I enjoyed a much-needed shower and good night's sleep. I was just grateful to be warm and out of the elements.

The next morning, I went back to the church at 9:45 to meet with the pastor at 10. I was standing outside, in the cold. The pastor came out at 10:15 and informed me that he would be available soon. I waited until he finally came back out at 11. We went inside to his office and chatted for a while and he began asking me theological questions to gauge the validity of my salvation. This puzzled me and we debated for several minutes. I knew that I was saved and that God had sent me on this journey. It was clear that we had some differences in our understanding, and I cordially ended the conversation by saying that we would have to agree to disagree.

I was a bit discouraged at how this meeting went, but my spirits were lifted when the pastor indicated that I could use church-owned property to spend the next night. However, my joy turned to disappointment when I learned that this property consisted of an empty field, 200 yards from the road. I would need to park my bike along the side of the road, walk through a field, and set up my tent next to the tree line. I thanked the pastor but knew that this would not work for me. The experience left me a little disillusioned because this is not the way I view the idea of Christian service and how the church of Jesus Christ should respond to a watching world.

As I left the church, doubts about this journey entered my mind. I was just starting out and things weren't going well. At this rate I would run out of money in a week. The church wouldn't help me, I couldn't get into a homeless shelter, and hotels were hard to find. Some used the pandemic as an excuse. "Lord, You told me you would provide..."

I began to ride and wondered, "What next?" Then the Lord spoke to me and said, "Pull over and talk to the policeman who is over there in his squad car." This was not something I wanted to do. Based on my past, I did not have the best relationship with law enforcement. But I needed to trust the Lord and what He had promised to do on this journey.

I pulled up beside the cruiser and the officer said, "Can I help you?" I told him who I was, where I was from, and what I was doing. "God said He would provide for me but no one will help." The officer directed me to a Biker church and said, "When you get there, ask for Bill Rae."

From the moment I arrived at Biker Church USA of Maine, I was family. A man named Paul greeted me and gave a handshake and a hug. I told him my story. He said, "Come inside. Are you hungry or thirsty, do you need a place to stay?" (These are words I would hear a lot on my journey!) The church put me up in a motel where they used to meet before they had a building. This church does so much to bless their community with the Gospel, and they did so much for me. I hung out at the church several times.

The next morning it was pouring rain and the forecast indicated more of the same for the entire day. I was discouraged and prayed, "Lord, You said if I ask I will receive and if I believe I will have. I am asking and believing that You will stop the rain so that I can do what I need to do, because I don't believe that You brought me here to sit in this motel room." I sensed the Lord speaking to me as I might talk to a close friend back home in Pennsylvania, "Boy, you ain't gonna melt; put on your raingear and go!" I argued a little with the Lord, but trusted what He was telling me. I continued to learn the lesson that God blesses our obedience.

I left and rode my bike in the pouring rain. There was no one around so I again questioned what I was doing. With all that had happened leading me up to this journey all I could think was, "I'm riding through the storm." Then I sensed a strong word from the Lord: "Jimmy, you are riding through the storm of your life, but I've got you, it will be okay. I want you to look for My beauty in the middle of the storm."

The words were comforting but all I could see around me was mud and rain. I sensed God telling me "Look to your left." I hadn't noticed it until then, but I looked left and the landscape opened up. I saw one of the most beautiful scenes I'd ever seen; a gorgeous river, flowing and glistening so peacefully, among trees with changing leaves. It took my breath away. The tears started to flow and I had to pull over because I couldn't see.

This place by the river is called "The Eddington Salmon Club." There was a roofed structure which looked like a back porch. I made my way up the steps and looked out over the river. I cried again, in awe of the river and beauty of God's creation. It seemed like He painted this picture just for me. I talked to Him, grateful for the moment. Then I heard His voice again, "Jimmy, make a Facebook live video and tell people about Me and the journey you're on." I continue to learn, but my nature is to push back, so I argued with God once more. I wondered why the God of the universe would be interested in social media. But I knew that He would bless my obedience so I made the video and called it, "Riding Through the Storm."

As of October 2021, more than 860 people had viewed that video. When I left the hotel that day, I had hoped to reach five, maybe ten people. God always has our best in mind, for His glory! You can view this video from 10/13/2020 by doing a Facebook search on, "Riding Through the Storm" or via this link:
https://tinyurl.com/JR-RidingThroughTheStorm

The following day was Wednesday and I was blessed to participate in a food distribution, sponsored by the church. I helped to direct traffic and hand out food to people who were struggling. That night I worshipped with my brothers and sisters at their Wednesday night service.

That same day I had visited a military surplus store. All throughout my journey I not only enjoyed the blessings of ministry but also experienced some amazing sights and places. There, I met a man named Paul Jr. in the parking lot. He was interested in my story so we talked. Interestingly, the security lights on my bike were blinking, which got his attention, so he came over to me. Miraculously, when he walked up to tell me that my lights were flashing, they stopped. This was another divine appointment!

Paul Jr. listened to my story and said, "You need to wait for my dad, he needs to hear this." His dad, Paul Sr., arrived shortly thereafter and listened to the story of my journey. He then handed me some money which I used for the next night's stay at the motel. Once again, God was meeting my needs.

The abundant blessings continued as the motel offered me a free stay for my third night. I had intended to

45

leave on Thursday morning since some bad weather was forecasted for Friday. However, something told me that God wanted me to remain a little longer. I prayed and felt God saying, "Yes, Jimmy, I've got more for you to do." So, I accepted the motel's offer for the free night's stay.

The next morning, I started on my way to a restaurant to get coffee, but for some reason I felt led to go back to my room. I figured that maybe I'd left something behind. I checked and everything was in order. Then I asked God what He wanted me to do today, and He said He would let me know. As I walked towards the parking lot, I ran into Tim from the biker church. He had actually pulled into the second motel entrance which is where I was. If I hadn't gone back to the room we never would have met. Tim said, "Do you have plans today?" I replied to Tim that I had just got done asking God what He wanted me to do today, and He told me He'd let me know. Tim responded, "I think He just did. I have a couple friends who might be encouraged by your story. Maybe you'd be willing to meet with them?" Of course, I saw this as another divine encounter and immediately agreed. I jumped into Tim's truck and off we went.

Tim's friend Kyle is retired from the Coast Guard. We talked for a while and shed a few tears together. A man had recently given Kyle some money as payment for work. Kyle did not want or need the money but he took it. The man had told Kyle, "If you don't want the money, someone will be coming along who can use it, give it to them." Kyle said to me, "That person is you." Kyle handed me the money and said, "You're that guy, Jimmy." This is just another of numerous examples of how God provided for me.

We then went to Jeff's place, (another one of Tim's friends), and I shared my journey with him also. After that, we went back to Tim's house where we had lunch. We had some red hot dogs named "Jordan's" and it reminded me of Jason's son, Jordan. I enjoyed those on some rolls that were split on the top instead of on the side like we had back home. Tim also gave me some of his homemade hot relish. It was amazing. Later that day I went for a bike ride with Tim and his wife, Darlene. The three of us rode around parts of Maine, sightseeing, and enjoying the awesome creation of God and a beautiful sunset.

I had spent a total of four days in Bangor, but it was time to move on. I woke up on Friday morning to pouring rain, which I experienced a great deal in the New England states. I travelled all day in the torrential rain to Massachusetts. If you're not a biker, you can't appreciate the danger and difficulty of riding in the rain. God protected me for sure! My time there laid a foundation for everything that happened on the remainder of the trip.

Sadly, Chris, the pastor of the biker church died on January 4, 2022 and his wife, Tracy, died a short time later on March 29, 2022. These two will be missed.

A "WICKED" AMAZING TIME
IN MASSACHUSETTS

My entire journey was filled with so many blessings and miracles that this book could not contain them all. Yet, certain experiences and places stand out and Massachusetts was one of those places.

After travelling all day, I arrived in Massachusetts late that evening. As was customary, I talked to the Lord and asked, "Where do I stay tonight?" Then the Lord told me, "Remember Bill Rae told you to google "biker church near me" if you needed help. The result came back quickly: "Broken Chains Biker Church" in Taunton, MA which was the closest thing to me.

I dialed the phone number from the website. After no one answered, I left a short message and stated that I was looking for help. I waited for about 20 minutes and there was no return call. I prayed again and sensed the Lord telling me to ride to the church. It was still pouring rain and would take about 40 minutes to get there. Aside from the difficult ride, I surmised that no one would be at the church—it was Friday night!

It was indeed a difficult ride, but I found the church and pulled into the parking lot. A man named Eric met me in the parking lot and approached my bike. "Man, you're dedicated," he said. All I could think of was my travels that day and how I was feeling, so I said, "I'm cold and wet, can you help me?" Eric responded, "Come on in and warm up." Once inside he said, "Take off that wet sweatshirt and here, have one of ours." Eric handed me a brand new "Broken Chains Biker Church" hoodie which was provided by "Big Dave" and his wife "Snowflake." I proudly still wear this sweatshirt almost every day.

Similar to what I experienced in Maine, Eric asked me if I needed food and drink, which I was grateful to get. He asked, "What else can we do for you?" I responded, "I'm looking for a place to stay tonight." Again, based on my current state, I responded, "I don't care where it is, just as long as it's out of the rain!" Eric said, "We can do better than that."

Eric called several men together and they huddled around me, praying for shelter. I remember that it was a simple prayer, something like, "Lord, where two or more are gathered, we know You're here. Please give our brother a warm place to stay, and we know that You will supply a nice warm bed for Jimmy to sleep in. Amen!"

My evening had just begun. To my amazement, this fellowship has church on Friday nights so that they can ride on Sundays to minister to the community and beyond. God had done it again; I don't know of any other church in Massachusetts that worships on a Friday night and He sent me there! You can't make this stuff up!

The service was amazing! It began with the playing of a Shofar and it sent chills down my spine. The next thing I heard was popular rock songs with Christian lyrics. It amazed me that songs I grew up with were being used to edify the Lord! The guest pastor, Reverend Art Warner, who wrote the book, Nuggets Gathered Along the Trail, preached a wonderful message that night. Interestingly, he preached the sermon from a pulpit which was built from a Springer front-end. It was so awesome and I thought to myself, *I would love to speak behind that someday*. Amazingly, I got to do just that as I shared my story on my second journey. God granted me that desire in a big way!

When the service was over, a woman named "Amy" approached me. "You're Jimmy, right?" She proceeded to hand me a set of keys. "These are the keys to my house. I'm staying with my daughter tonight and you're spending the night at my house." She pointed at me and said, "You're going to stay at my house tonight. You're going to get a shower, sleep in my bed, eat my food, drink my drinks, and take anything you need for your journey." I was blown away! Who does this? Here was a single mother who was giving her home and its contents to a perfect stranger for the night. What a heart for God and people!

I followed Amy back to her house after church. She took me inside and showed me around her house. As she was leaving, she said, "Just put the key under this rock if you're gone before I get back the next morning."

I learned later that there was more to this story. You see, Amy was the one who got my message when I originally called the church. She talked to several church leaders and members but no one knew what to do with my request for help. She thought about ignoring the message but then I showed up in church. During the Friday evening service, Amy prayed and asked for God's direction. The Lord placed it on her heart to let me stay at her place. Once again, obedience resulted in a blessing, not only to me, but to Amy as well. I got a wonderful shower and a good night's sleep at Amy's house and left the next morning.

I headed to the northwest corner of the U.S.

**The Springer front-end pulpit at Broken Chains
Biker Church**

A dream come true as I got to share my journey from the pulpit months later

AN UNEXPECTED STOP IN THE BUCKEYE STATE

I learned so many lessons on my journey and God continues to teach me. One thing I've learned is that I made my plans, but time and time again, God provided "holy interruptions." Such was the case as I made my way towards Washington state.

My route to the west took me through New York state once again. I noticed a sign for Niagara Falls and felt led to make a stop there. The Falls would be a blessing to see but I also knew that there would be people there for me to talk to, encourage, and share the love of Jesus. I was slightly disappointed when I pulled up to the entrance gate and saw the price to park at the Falls. It was more than I wanted to pay, so I decided to look for a way out and get back on the road. But there was no direct way out without first going through the gate. I wasn't sure what I was going to do. But once again, God had a plan and amazed me!

A woman, who I later learned was named Amanda, had just parked her car about 30 yards away. Somehow, she noticed me sitting at the gate and walked towards me. Without saying a word, she took her credit card and "swiped" me in, which took care of my parking fee. She walked back to her car without saying a word.

I rode over to her car, thanked her, and shared the story of my journey with her. As I love to do, I also took a picture with her as a memory to her kindness and generosity. After that, I walked around the Falls and took in the majesty and beauty of God's awesome creation. God brought several people across my path, but I spent extended time with one special couple, Ed and Dawn. Ed and Dawn are bikers like me and they were dressed in Harley gear. After we chatted and I shared my journey with them, these new friends blessed me with a gift card from the Cheesecake Factory. Niagara Falls was indeed a "holy interruption." I got back on the road and eventually made my way to Ohio.

Things were going fine until my bike started acting up. As an auto mechanic by trade, I recognized the symptoms: my clutch was failing. I pulled off to the side of the highway and put the bike in neutral. The clutch felt fine but when I let it out, the bike would not move. It was getting dark and raining. Now what should I do? Then I realized that God had already handled this provision as well.

Before I had left Pennsylvania to start on my journey, I stopped by my chiropractor's office to give one of the employees a birthday card. I just love spreading the love of Jesus through kind gestures. With all He has done for me, He has given me a heart for people. For some reason, the doors to the office were locked and the business was closed that day. I was puzzled but needed to run other errands.

I didn't plan on it, but decided to stop in and see my insurance agent since that office is close to the chiropractor's. My agent, Karen, is also a believer so I told her about the journey I was about to embark on. I assumed that she would be interested in what God was doing! Karen asked, "Jimmy, will you be using your pickup trucks while you're away?" I said that the trucks would sit unused at my house. She said, "Let's do this: we will reduce the insurance on your trucks to the bare minimum and place coverage on your bike, to include roadside assistance and trip interruption." Amazingly, this also lowered the total cost of my insurance, which was another blessing! I was grateful for her expertise; I never would have thought to do this. I did not expect to need to use this coverage, at the time. Who knew that the actions by my agent would lead to more unexpected "God sightings?"

As I sat on the side of the highway, God reminded me that my insurance now included roadside assistance. I called the insurance company and they arranged to have a tow truck sent to my location.

The tow truck turned out to be a rollback, driven by a man named "Chris." Chris arrived and confirmed my diagnosis: it had to be the clutch because the bike would not move. The challenge was getting the bike safely onto the rollback as it was heavily overloaded with all my gear. I sat on the bike and we tried to walk it up the ramp. After some tricky moments, we got the bike loaded up and strapped down.

I knew that God had orchestrated this divine encounter, starting back in Pennsylvania with my insurance agent. For the entire trip to the garage, I told Chris about Jesus and my journey. I don't know if Chris had experienced the love of Jesus because he asked me, "Jimmy, why does God allow bad things to happen to good people?" Chris shared a terrible incident with me that happened with one of his close family members. "Why did God allow that to happen, Jimmy?" I didn't have a good answer but prayed silently. What came to mind were these words: "What Satan means for evil God intended for good. I believe that your family member will be used someday by God." Chris was open to these words and his heart was softened.

We arrived at the garage and nearly dropped the bike as I attempted to remove it from the rollback. As I unloaded the bike and put it in gear, it wouldn't move, confirming what I experienced on the highway. Chris gave me the name of two garages which could diagnose and repair motorcycles. I planned to call in the morning. For now, I walked to a hotel across the street to get a good night's sleep. My insurance not only covered the tow but also the hotel and meals during the time my bike was being repaired. I thought about the expense this would have been without the God-inspired visit to my insurance agent. I thanked God for His amazing provision and enjoyed a sweet sleep.

In the morning, I dialed the first number Chris had given me and there was no answer. I dialed the second number and the owner of Fountain City Cycles answered. His name is Ralph. I explained a little bit about my journey and told him that the clutch on my bike had gone out. Ralph informed me that he would drive to the garage where I was and be there in 30 minutes. He actually closed up his shop and drove 11 miles with his enclosed trailer to help me out.

Ralph walked in with a big smile and strangely said, "She won't move at all, huh," as if he knew something I didn't. He got on the bike, started it up, and drove it onto the trailer. This made no sense. It wouldn't move on the highway and Chris confirmed it. Ralph said that he would take the bike back to his shop and look it over.

Ralph rode the bike all over town and tore it apart, looking for any problems. He could not find anything wrong with it. He adjusted a nut which was secured too tightly, in his opinion, but this would not have caused the issue I experienced. Ralph drove his car from his shop to my hotel. He picked me up and drove me back to the shop. Ralph had spent hours working on my bike and test driving it. In total he had driven 44 miles back and forth to help me out. He also installed a new battery in my key fob. I was rightfully prepared for a large bill, but Ralph charged me $93 for everything. I protested because I knew how much time he had spent on my bike. But he would hear none of it. "Jimmy,

I love what you are doing, that's all I'm charging," he said. I later posted this story on Facebook and friends donated $100 to my bank account which covered my bike and a little more. You'll hear me say this a lot, but this was one more example of how God took care of me, providing abundantly more than I needed!

Back at the hotel I had a delicious dinner which was covered by my insurance. My server's name was "Maddie." She was friendly, attentive, and did a great job. During the meal, I couldn't help but notice an interesting tattoo on Maddie's wrist. I asked her about it and she told me that it was a "Suicide Awareness" tattoo. When Maddie told me that, I asked if I could share my story with her and she was eager to hear it. We cried together and the blessings were mutual. I keep in contact with Maddie to this day. In fact, I try to keep in touch with Maddie, Chris, and many others who God placed in my path on the journey.

I spent almost two days in Montpelier, Ohio on an unplanned visit. I don't understand why my clutch did what it did, but I believe it was because God wanted me to talk with Chris and Maddie. The blessings on this journey just kept on coming.

LIL WOLF

Amy had told me about a guy named "Lil Wolf" who lived in Ohio. She suggested that I contact him, and meet with him, if I ever had the chance, because he was a great guy and servant of the Lord.

Amy had given me Lil Wolf's number so I called him when my bike had broken down in Montpelier. He planned to call me back if he could find help but I got ahold of Ralph first. When Lil Wolf did call me back, Ralph was already taking care of me.

While Ralph was diagnosing my bike, the Lord laid Lil Wolf on my heart so I called him again and asked if I could visit. Lil Wolf was about three hours from where I was but I knew that I wanted to meet him and see what the Lord had in store.

When I got close to Lil Wolf's address my GPS took me to a long dirt lane through a cornfield. I wondered if I had made a wrong turn or if my GPS had led me down a wrong road. But eventually I came to a clearing which revealed a house, a garage, and a barn. I know that we can't accurately assess anyone based on looks alone, but Lil Wolf just looked like the epitome of a biker to me.

You need to understand that Lil Wolf is a "1%er" Outlaw. He is also the chaplain of the Outlaw Motorcycle Club. Lil Wolf was imprisoned for a long period of time. Upon his release, he was led to the Lord by an ex-Hell's Angel. He has a ministry called "Lil Wolf Ministries" which is focused on leading others to Jesus. As chaplain of the club, he rides his bikes all over the country to perform weddings and funerals. I cannot overstate the impact Lil Wolf had on my journey. The connections he made led to every other connection throughout the country. Without his support, my journey would not have been possible.

He led me into the house which actually belonged to a married couple, Hoss and his wife Voodoo. Lil Wolf shared his testimony with me and we hung out together. Eventually Hoss and Voodoo came home from work. Hoss is a Black Piston, which is a support club for the Outlaws. He is a big man with an even bigger heart. He and Voodoo hosted me for dinner and invited me to stay for as long as I needed to.

I was concerned about winter weather in the Midwest and western states so I wanted to get on the road. Hoss gave me a pair of gloves to keep me warm on my journey. Lil Wolf provided some financial support which was always needed and appreciated. He also gave me two of his ministry shirts and prayed with me before I left.

Lastly, Lil Wolf said to me, "Put Mike's number in your phone and call him when you get to Missouri." Mike is with the Tribe of Judah Motorcycle Ministry and would prove to be another great blessing to me in the remainder of my journey.

As I left Hoss and Voodoo's place and headed to Missouri on the interstate, I looked to my left and noticed something interesting; a man in the passenger seat of an SUV was holding up a device which appeared to be an iPad, pointed in my direction. I wasn't sure if he was taking a picture or a video, but we exchanged smiles. I gave the peace sign and kept driving. I can't tell you how many times I received smiles, waves and "thumbs up" along my journey. I thought to myself, "I would love to be able to talk to him about what I'm doing on the road." An hour or two later, after many miles had passed, I got off the interstate for gas.

There were two gas stations to choose from, but I felt led to pick the one on the right.

I quickly learned why the Lord prompted me to select that particular gas station. As I was filling my bike with fuel, the same man with the iPad approached me. "Coincidentally," he had pulled into the same gas station I chose. I learned that his name is "Montana" and I realized that my prayer on the interstate was answered; I had the opportunity to tell Montana what I was doing on my journey. He excitedly said, "You have to meet my wife and mother." I walked over to their SUV and told them about my journey which they were excited to hear about. This was one more divine appointment arranged by the Lord. Like many others I met along the way, Montana and I keep in touch on social media to this day.

Picture taken by my new friend, Montana, from his SUV. The "stuff" I carried always made people curious!

STOPS IN MISSOURI AND OKLAHOMA

When I arrived in Missouri, it was dark and raining. These seemed to be the typical conditions whenever I arrived at a new destination. I stopped at a gas station and called Mike as Lil Wolf had recommended. While I waited for Mike to arrive, I encountered a woman stocking shelves in the convenience store. This was another God-established opportunity to talk about Jesus so I approached her and shared my story.

Shortly after I had called Mike, he came into the store and we greeted each other. He invited me to supper and I gratefully accepted his invitation. Mike was driving a large SUV and I followed his vehicle to a Mexican restaurant. As I parked, I noticed several people exiting the SUV. Mike's wife, daughter, and grandson had accompanied him to the restaurant.

I said to Mike, "I didn't realize you were bringing your entire family?" Mike responded that it was his birthday and his family was taking him out to celebrate. I felt like a third wheel and said to Mike, "Why don't we do this another time, enjoy spending your birthday with your family." Mike would hear none of it. "No, we want you here. This is awesome, I get to do ministry work on my birthday!"

What followed was just one more example of God's goodness and provision. Mike graciously paid for my dinner and we walked out of the restaurant. Before he got into his vehicle he said, "Follow me, we got you a room for the night." Mike had booked me into a nice hotel for the night. I was carrying a good deal of stuff on my bike and Mike insisted on helping me carry my belongings inside. As he left Mike said, "I'll be back at 8 tomorrow morning. We'll go to breakfast and talk some more."

As promised, Mike showed up the next day at 8 a.m. sharp. I had a great breakfast with his family and once again, Mike took care of the bill. He got serious for a moment and let me know that he and his wife, Erin, were concerned about my travel plans because the forecast was calling for bad weather. "Jimmy, I'd like you to stay in the Tribe of Judah clubhouse all week until the weather clears on Friday." I was so moved by Mike's concern for me and I felt confirmation from the Lord that this was what I should do. Shortly after that, Erin came into the clubhouse with two armfuls of groceries. There was enough there for the rest of the week. I sincerely asked her, "What do I owe you?" Her reply was, "Nothing Jimmy, we'll take care of you." I was not only blown away at my friends' generosity, but also for the miraculous way that God was continuously taking care of me. This wonderful couple provided for all of my needs. Mike even picked me up after work a few times, fed me, and allowed me to use their shower and laundry. I was also blessed to attend church with Mike and his family. The pastor of their church generously gave me several gift cards to support me along my journey.

The clubhouse was heated by an outside wood burner. In order to keep warm, I estimate that I burned half of their woodpile during my stay. Mike and his wife refused to take anything for it. They insisted that I was doing the Lord's work and they wanted to be a part of it. Mike said, "Perhaps someday, if you have extra money, maybe you can make a donation to our ministry." I pray that God would grow my ministry and allow me to do that one day.

One day when I was standing outside, a young man named "Shane" and his dad "Nick" approached me at the clubhouse. I felt led to tell them about my journey. Nick said, "Oh, you're one of them." I was taken aback, and just being honest with you, a little angry at his comment. But Nick had said this "tongue-in-cheek;" I learned later that he and Shane were both believers. Nick wanted to see my bike and he enthusiastically sat on it. We hit it off and became instant friends.

Shane sent me a message which said, "Dad would like to invite you to supper on Sunday," which turned out to be the Sunday family meal. Evidently, Shane and Nick had spread the word to their family about my journey and there

67

was a full house at the meal! I sat beside Matt, Shane's brother. I won't get into the details, but Matt was struggling and needed encouragement. I am so grateful that I was able to spend time with and pray for Matt. When I left, Nick handed me a cool rechargeable flashlight as a gift. He patted my coat and told me to check the pocket when I returned to the clubhouse. Once again, God had provided through this loving family.

During the week Nick got the idea that he and I needed to make something tangible for my journey. Nick had the material and tools to allow us to be creative. We decided to make a cross which would be a memento of my journey and the time I spent with them. This cross was displayed on my bike for the rest of the journey and is still attached to my handlebars to this day. Not only does it remind me of the sacrifice Jesus made for me, but also serves as a witness to everyone I encounter that I belong to Him.

I said my goodbyes to Mike and family and got ready to continue my ride to Washington state. I still hear from Mike every day. My plans never included an extended stay in Missouri but God's ways are not my ways. I spent about a week there, filled with divine encounters and blessings which characterized my entire journey.

OKLAHOMA

The Sooner State was never part of my planned route to Washington. All along, I intended to take a northern route, to include I-80, for my ride to the northwest corner of the U.S. This was the quickest, most direct route to Washington. But back in Ohio, Lil Wolf told me that this was a bad idea. Looking back, I know that God was speaking through this man.

Lil Wolf travels the country on a Heritage Softail, or if needed, on a Harley trike with a trailer in tow. He honors deceased bikers with their "last ride," and his trailer doubles as a hearse. Based on his experience and knowledge of weather conditions at that time of year, Lil Wolf strongly suggested that I take a more southern route via I-40. And so here I was in Oklahoma. Even though this state was never part of my plan, it was part of God's!

When I left Missouri, Mike gave me the number of a man named "Rex," who is a member of the "Brothers Forgiven Motorcycle Ministry." Mike told me to call Rex when I got to Oklahoma. When I got close to Tulsa, I called Rex as Mike had suggested. Rex was expecting my call and gave me the address where I could meet him. Soon after that, I arrived at the barber shop he owns and runs.

I talked with Rex and shared testimonies with him and two other guys at his business. Once he closed up shop for the day we went to dinner at a local steakhouse and met up with a man named "Skoot." Skoot is a college professor and also a member of the Brothers Forgiven Motorcycle

69

Ministry. Skoot generously paid for everyone's meal and he and Rex blessed my bike and gave me several gifts.

The plan was for me to follow Skoot and Rex to my hotel where they would see me off for the night. Skoot graciously put me up for two nights at the hotel. He and Rex had plans to see a man named "Spur" who is with the Outlaws Motorcycle Club in Oklahoma. We arrived at the hotel and my new friends helped carry my personal belongings inside.

As Skoot and Rex were saying their goodbyes to me, Skoot said to me, "Change in plans, Spur wants to meet you." You need to understand that visits to the clubhouse were by invitation only and I wasn't comfortable with the idea of going there; I didn't know what to expect and thought that it was best if I didn't go. Skoot reassured me and said, "Spur is a good guy, you'll be okay." After unloading my gear at the hotel, I found myself at the clubhouse, face-to-face with Spur.

When I got my first look at Spur, I noticed that he was a wearing a long-sleeve shirt with writing on the sleeve. From the best I could tell, the inscription looked something like, "Jesus Saves." Wow, could this man be a Christian? Again, God had provided another brother in Christ.

I discovered that club members come from all walks of life and are not the stereotypical people often portrayed by the media. I cannot say enough about Spur; he is one of the nicest, most real men I've ever met. His assistance and connections helped me for the rest of my journey and beyond. The two of us spent about an hour and a half sitting on the couch, sharing our testimonies. With a handshake and biker hug we said goodbye and I went back to the hotel.

At the hotel, I shared the story of my journey with the ladies at the front desk and headed to the room. Before I turned out the lights I thought about my precious daughter, Heavyn. I was reminded of her when I saw my little monkey named "Bogey." This stuffed animal was mine as a child, and I passed it on to Heavyn when she was little. I now kept it with me on my journey as a reminder of her. That night, I took a picture of Bogey and sent it to Heavyn in a text message, letting her know that I took a part of her along on my journey. I then drifted off into a sweet sleep.

On the second day in Oklahoma, Spur called me. He told me that the Heavenly Father had spoken to him after we had parted company on the previous night. He felt the Lord telling him to help me get around the country for the remainder of my journey. Spur asked me, "Would you be okay with that?" I didn't have to think long. I responded, "If God is calling you to do that, I'll take it!"

Spur helped me for the rest of my journey. I heard from him every day. The typical conversation began with Spur asking, "Where are you at tonight?" When I would tell Spur where I would be settling for the night, he would say something like, "Give me a little bit." Without fail, he would either call or text back shortly with the name and number of a contact in the area. When I would call, the person on the other end would say, "Spur said you'd be calling, I'll call or text my address to you." And this is how it went for the rest of my journey; he tried to secure accommodations for me as often as he could and he succeeded many times.

Bikers are family and take care of each other and others. To this day, I still hear from Spur every single day. All glory goes to God for orchestrating this!

That same day, Rex took me on a ride through parts of Oklahoma to experience the beauty of God's creation. We ended up at a local ice cream restaurant to get some food. While Rex and I were seated at the table enjoying lunch, I noticed a tall black gentleman walking in with two women. As happened so often on my journey, I sensed God speaking, telling me to go and talk with the man. "Tell him your story, about your time with the KKK, and what I (the Lord) have done in your life." As I've done before, I argued with God. "This man is much bigger than me and may not take too kindly to that information, Lord!" But I kept hearing God saying, "Go, Jimmy." So, I stepped out in faith and approached the table.

At the table, I met Chris, Juanita, and Denise and asked, "How are you doing?" Chris said something like, "We're blessed," which gave me a hint that he might be a follower of Jesus. I learned that they were indeed believers and I got to share my journey, my past with the KKK, and how God rescued me. We ended our conversation and remain friends on social media to this day. The mutual blessings were just another example of the divine appointments set up by our amazing God! After Rex and I left the restaurant we continued the amazing ride, taking in the beautiful sights.

On my final day at the hotel, Skoot contacted the Brother-to-Brother Biker Church and told the pastor about my journey. The pastor invited me to speak at the Saturday evening service. I was blessed to do so and rode to the church which was not far from where I had been staying.

At the service, I spoke about my journey and all that God had done for me. It was a memorable evening! At the close of the service, preacher Dennis announced to the congregation that there was a hat in the front of the sanctuary and that anyone felt led to do so could donate to my journey. I told the congregation that I didn't come to speak for money, I came to talk about Jesus. Preacher Dennis responded, "We understand that brother, but we want to bless you and be a part of your journey. Please don't steal our blessing." I was humbled at the heart of this church and what God was doing. He handed me a wad of money which I did not count until I returned to the hotel. When I unraveled the ball of money I was floored by the size of their gift. I am so grateful for the church's generosity and the blessing I received from being a part of their fellowship that evening. And I also hear from preacher Dennis almost every day which is a great blessing to me!

Before I left Oklahoma, I called back to Pennsylvania to pay for my life insurance. God arranged another divine appointment as I got to share my journey with an agent. Shortly after that, I found a Facebook group called, "Riding Through Oklahoma." I left a post to let people know how much I appreciated the beauty in Oklahoma. One member of the group replied to me and asked if I had ever heard of the "Bunk-A-Biker" site. I decided to check out the site which has a helpful map that allows you to zoom in to any location. The site then displays location "pins" for individuals who provide accommodations and support for

73

bikers. I used this site numerous times during my journey and it blessed me tremendously!

I left Oklahoma on November 2, 2020 and continued on my southern route to Washington. Rex, Skoot, Spur, and several others provided so many lasting blessings while I was there. Sadly, Rex went home be with the Lord on February 11, 2021 but his memory will be with me always.

Lil Wolf in action

The cross Nick and I made together

The cross as it sits on my handlebars to this day

Bogey, my sidekick and reminder of Heavyn

TAKING A SOUTHERN ROUTE
TO GO NORTH

Based on Lil Wolf's concerns and advice, I came into the Lone Star State after the wonderful experiences in Oklahoma. By taking this southern route my goal was to avoid winter weather, namely snow and ice. My time in Texas was relatively brief, but God had people for me to meet, as He always did along this journey.

Lil Wolf and Hoss had told me to see "Miss Brenda" at the Midway Café when I passed through Adrian, Texas. They highly recommended the fried bologna sandwich. I obliged and the sandwich was amazing! I also had a slice of Tennessee whiskey chocolate pecan pie which was great too. Brenda told me that she loves Lil Wolf and Hoss, who (like me now) are always welcome there. When I went to pay, Brenda not only took care of my bill, but also handed me some money to help me out. God continued to amaze me through the generosity and blessings of His people.

Eventually I stopped at a gas station and met a man named Jeff. Jeff was with the Christian Soldiers Clean and Sober Motorcycle Ministry and he walked up to me and my bike. He said, "This is going to sound crazy but God told me to give you this," and he slipped some cash into my hand. I chuckled, which at first startled Jeff. He may have thought that I was being sarcastic but I was actually just in awe once again of God's provision. I explained to Jeff that his gesture was not crazy at all, this is just what God had been doing from the start of my journey. It is what He promised to do.

In the course of time, I saw a sign, "Grand Canyon, 10 miles." I didn't realize that I would ever be so close to this wonder. I'd never seen the Grand Canyon and wondered if God might be okay with me taking a side trip to experience it? I lifted my eyes towards Heaven but before I could ask, I sensed God's voice saying, "Go ahead and go, son, there are people there for you to talk to." I started to cry and had to pull over when the tears distorted my vision. I was in awe of God's goodness once again.

When I got off of the exit, I noticed a sign for an attraction called, "Bearizona." I wanted to visit but by that time it was closing. When I arrived at the Grand Canyon, darkness had set in so I found a nearby room for the night. I spoke to the woman at the front desk about my journey.

The next morning, I rode to the entrance of the canyon and noticed that the entry fee was $30. I struggled for a moment with the cost, but surmised that the money I had came from the Lord, and He had directed me here at this point in time. I asked the park ranger how long it would take me to ride through and he indicated 2 – 3 hours. From the moment I arrived, I was in awe of God's handiwork. I pulled over at the first lookout and went to the edge. I cried once again. There is no way you can look at the Grand Canyon and not see God's handiwork. I visited every lookout point and talked to many people about my journey and the Lord.

When I left the Grand Canyon, I proceeded to Bearizona to check it out. This wasn't a planned part of my trip but God knows how much I love wildlife. My purpose on this journey was to ride and tell people about Jesus, but He also gave me the other desires of my heart as well.

At the entrance I was told that I could not ride my bike through the park because I would be vulnerable to bear attacks. I was disappointed, but was told that I could use a walking path to view bears in pens. The employee took pity on me and did not make me pay the entry fee since I couldn't ride through the park. As I walked on the sidewalk a nice lady named "Jen" came over to me. "Did you park a motorcycle out front?" she asked. "We got word that someone snuck in the back way." I told Jen about my journey and that I was not permitted to take my bike into the park. She said, "Come with me," so I followed.

What happened next was yet another example of God's goodness. Jen handed me the keys to the company Jeep and told me to drive through and enjoy myself in the park. She did not charge me a cent. Who does this?! I had an amazing time at this awesome park. When I completed the tour, an employee named John directed me to the spot where I could park the vehicle. And I was able to share my journey with him and several others that I met there. I can't begin to express my gratitude for the phenomenal people I encountered along the way to the four corners of the U.S.!

I spent the night in Kingman, Arizona and used Bunk-A-Biker to locate accommodations provided by a woman named "Barbara." Barbara met me at a local store and led me back to her house. She insisted that I park my bike under her carport, out of the elements, while her car sat out. She made dinner for me and we talked until the wee hours about the amazing love and goodness of Jesus. Barbara is a strong believer and played videos of her favorite pastors and clips from their sermons. In the morning, she made me breakfast, packed a lunch for my ride, and gave me the gift of a military can opener to use on my journey. I had a great time with Barbara and am so thankful for her kindness and hospitality.

I left Barbara's house and stopped for gas at the Route 66 Canada Gas Station. It was there where I met Dianna and Marjorie. Initially they were afraid to talk to me, but they soon approached me and I told them my story. They gave me a donation and we became friends on social media, where they followed my journey.

Barbara had recommended that I take "The Mojave Rattlesnake," a ten-mile section of old Route 66. This road has 222 turns and makes for a great ride in the desert. In my experience, I prefer roads like this to those which are straight and monotonous.

After the exciting ride through the desert, I came out in Oatman, Arizona, a touristy old west town with a history of gold mining. I met up with a man named

"Grizzly." He had passed me earlier on Route 66 and I noticed the cool bike he had. I just loved his bike! It had elk and mule deer horns, and other references to wildlife. Grizzly runs a charity for animals. I talked to him for a while about my journey and the Lord. "Coincidentally," I would run into him later in Daytona. For now, I was headed to California via Nevada.

NEVADA AND CALIFORNIA

On my way to the Golden State, Spur called to find out where I was headed and what I needed. I told him that my bike would soon need regular maintenance, including an oil change. He gave me the number for a man named "Russell" who lived in Nevada. Russell was part of the Soldiers for Jesus Motorcycle Club.

When I got to the area where Russell lived, I called him and described my situation. Russell told me to call a man named "Kenny" at Boulder Choppers motorcycle repair shop. Kenny is also a member of Soldiers for Jesus. It was Friday at 3 p.m. when I called Kenny. Given my experience as a mechanic, I didn't expect Kenny to get to my bike on a Friday afternoon. But Kenny told me to bring the bike over. I rode the bike to Kenny's shop and up onto the lift. Once my bike was strapped down and in the air, Kenny said, "You need a back tire!" I disagreed and said, "It still has a few miles left on it." My only goal was to have the bike checked out and the oil changed. But as was the case throughout my journey, God had other plans.

Kenny then said, "Can you stay until tomorrow? You're coming home with me." Kenny stopped to pick up some dinner for the two of us and his wife, Jennifer. We all sat down to a great meal at Kenny's house. Then I spent a great night getting to know Kenny and his family. They showed me to my room and I was able to get a nice shower. I had a great night's sleep.

The next morning, Kenny took me out to breakfast where Russell and some of the other club guys joined us. For whatever reason, the group insisted that I order a huge omelet meal. I didn't want to consume such a big breakfast, but the guys wanted to see me tackle it. "You're a big man, you can handle it," they said with a smile. I finally agreed, but it took all of my effort to finish the massive platter.

After breakfast we went to the shop. Before Kenny installed the new back tire, he discovered that I needed new brake pads. A coworker drove me to a local Harley dealer to buy the pads. Once we got back to the shop, we put the bike back together.

As the bike came down from the lift, I asked Kenny what I owed him. He would not take a dime from me. Kenny said, "Nothing, just keep doing what you're doing." Thinking about it now, I would estimate that the parts and labor would have cost at least $500. Once again, I stood in awe of how God was providing for me, through generous people like Kenny.

Before I left Nevada, Kenny gave me the number of a man named J.D. in Bakersfield, California. J.D., like Russell, was part of the Soldiers for Jesus Motorcycle Club.

84

When I arrived in Bakersfield and contacted J.D., he gave me a place to stay in the spare bedroom of his home. The next morning, J.D.'s wife fixed a big breakfast for me. We hung out for a while and then J.D. took me back to his garage. He gave me a new set of handguards and installed them on my bike. He then had a puzzled look as he noticed the hair ties on my throttle. I used those as a crude cruise control on the bike. J.D. said, "Get those off of there!" He gave me a throttle lock which is a much better, more appropriate cruise control device. He also handed me a generous amount of cash for my journey. I thanked him for his generosity and fellowship and was on the road once again.

Back on the interstate I noticed that my clutch was slipping when the bike was in third gear. I tried to call J.D. for help but he was in church. Then the Lord reminded me to do an internet search on "biker church near me." This was the resource which helped me out back in Massachusetts. I found a phone number and dialed it. A man answered and invited me to his home. We tinkered around with the bike but could not fix the issue. I thanked him and got back on the road.

I used the Bunk-A-Biker site to find a place to stay but quickly realized that the ride to the house would be challenging. I started up a mountain where rain turned to snow, sleet, and freezing rain. Traffic was heavy and I found myself in the third (fast) lane of the highway. My goggles fogged up and I removed them, basically driving with one hand. I put my signal on, attempting to ease over into the far-right lane to find an exit, but no one would let me merge.

I pleaded with God to help me find an exit where I could get off of the interstate and into some type of shelter.

I had no choice but to squeeze over and hope that the car beside me would slow down, allowing me to change lanes. When I looked in my right-side mirror and saw the car's headlights go down, I recognized that they were braking, making it safe for me to change lanes. I can't describe just how treacherous it was driving in these conditions. Miraculously, as soon as I was able to get into the right (slow) lane, there was an exit! I praised God for this! Just a short distance up the road I found a gas station.

I did not have the right gear and clothing for the weather I was experiencing. I was frozen to the bone and spent some time in the restroom, warming my cold hands under the hand dryer. When I was slightly thawed out, I went to the checkout counter and said to the clerk, "I'm in a bit of a pickle and need some help. I need a warm place to stay tonight. Any recommendations?" The clerk said, "You can't see it from here but there is a motel about 200 yards up the road. I suggest that you stay there because this snow isn't stopping anytime soon." I was so grateful that God had protected me and provided yet another refuge in the storm for me!

When I pulled up to the hotel, a woman was standing at the front door and yelled to me, "Hey, are you staying here tonight?" I indicated that I was. She said, "Pull your bike under the canopy, it's too pretty to be out in the snow." This employee allowed me to park my bike right at the entrance to the hotel, protected from the snow. I felt so undeserving and humbled as I noticed several other bikes in the parking lot, all covered in snow. I was so grateful for this blessing from God and the fact that the hotel had vacancies. I spoke to this woman at the front desk for over an hour about my journey and the Lord. And amazingly, not a person could enter or leave the hotel without seeing my bike, the cross, and numerous references to Jesus! This led to several encounters and opportunities to talk about my Lord and Savior!

By 10 a.m. the next morning, the roads were clear enough that I could continue on my journey north through California. That evening, as I did many evenings, I used the Bunk-A-Biker site to find a place to stay. I contacted Greg and Amanda who invited me to their house. One of the highlights was holding Greg's albino Texas Rat snake. I love snakes!

At that point my bike was still functional but I had to really baby the clutch. It needed to be fixed sooner rather than later. Greg knew of a good garage and said we would go there first thing in the morning.

The next day Greg took me to the garage, as promised. I was told that they would get to my bike when they could if I would leave it at the garage. That was my best option so I left the bike and walked about a mile to a restaurant for breakfast. At the restaurant I had the opportunity to talk with several customers and staff members about my journey.

While I was still at the restaurant, the garage called to inform me that they had a cancellation. They had my bike torn apart and asked if I could return to the garage. I walked the mile back to the garage where I learned that my clutch was fried. My voltage regulator also needed to be replaced. The parts and labor would cost $1200 to fix. I called Greg and asked if I could stay another night, wondering how the Lord would provide for me with the cost of the bike repair. I intended to walk back to Greg's house but he took the rest of the day off from work and picked me up. That was so gracious of Greg to do that and I was grateful for his kindness.

After pondering what to do, I decided to write a Facebook post, telling people about my situation. I posted something like, "I don't know how God will take care of it but I can't wait to see how He will do it." To my amazement (I say this because I never want to lose the wonder of how awesome God is), in less than four hours over $1300 had been electronically deposited to my bank account. The bike was fixed the next day and I was able to get back on the road. Once again, God had abundantly provided, just as He promised when He called me to this journey.

A friend Lori gave me a quote that is appropriate here and throughout my journey: "When my God shows up, He shows off." This is how we know it's Him.

As I said at the beginning of this story, you can't look at my journey and not see God in it. At this time, a man I had never met, Stacy, sent me a Facebook message. He stated, "You don't know me but I believe in what you are doing. Can I help by giving you a donation?" I was grateful for the help and said, "Yes, if that is what God is calling you to do." He sent a generous gift which helped me to continue on my journey. My cousin Crissy had told Stacy about my journey; he was intrigued by it and wanted to help. One of my old friends, Buddy, messaged me and asked if I had enough to cover repairs. I was still a good bit short and Buddy graciously said, "Consider it done." He sent the funds within five minutes and once again God had provided. There are so many stories like this, I wish I had the space to mention them all. But the bottom line is this: it was all God's doing and He alone gets the glory!

THE SECOND CORNER

ALONG THE PACIFIC COAST

As I made my way towards the second corner of the U.S. I arrived in Coos Bay, Oregon. It was nearing evening so I found Gary and Joni through the Bunk-A-Biker site. These generous people invited me to their house. When I arrived at the address, Joni met me at the end of their long driveway. Gary and Joni provided me with a shower and a nice bed for the evening.

When I woke up the next morning, I could hardly move my left arm. The positioning of my arms on the long ride across the country was causing severe pain. Still, if I picked up my left arm with my right hand, I believed that I could continue riding. I wanted to continue to the second corner, but Joni would have none of it. She insisted that I get medical attention so she took me to a local Urgent Care.

At the conclusion of my exam, Joni asked for the paperwork so that she could review it. Honestly, she treated me like a caring mother would. After she read the paperwork and diagnosis, she lovingly said, "Get comfy, you are not going anywhere for at least three days." Joni drove me around to pick up my prescription and a Transcutaneous Electrical Nerve (TENS) unit to alleviate the pain in my arm. She and Gary insisted that I take it easy and they allowed me to stay in their house, even when they were not there. They fed me and allowed me to use their shower, laundry, and anything I needed. They were so trusting and treated me like family.

God sent me to a lot of Christians on my journey. Gary and Joni are examples of what it means to be Christ-like. They didn't just love with words but with their actions as well. I had the privilege of attending church with them. I was also blessed to spend time with them cleaning the church, and I helped Gary install a metal roof on his shed. As I prepared to leave this amazing couple, Gary gave me a full-face helmet as a gift. This would protect me from the rainy weather I would encounter as I continued to Washington state.

As I continued to head north through Oregon, I asked the question which had become customary: "Lord, where am I staying tonight?" The Bunk House Motel was the answer for that evening. I pulled into the parking lot and went to the office to see about a room. I met the owner, Nick, and we started talking. I learned that a room was available and I laid the $60 fee on the counter. Nick, like several others in the area, wondered why I was undertaking this journey at this time of year, given the unpredictable weather. Seriously, I think people thought that I had taken leave of my senses. But after we had talked for a while, and Nick heard my story, his heart softened. He went to a freezer and pulled out a frozen dinner. He handed me the dinner along with my $60. He told me to enjoy a good night's sleep and dinner, on him. I microwaved the frozen dinner and slept well that night. God had done it again! I was back on the road the next morning.

THE EVERGREEN STATE – MY SECOND CORNER

As I reflect on my journey, the overall goal was to ride to the four corners of the United States and tell people about Jesus. So much of this story happened along the way. It's ironic that my time at the second corner of the U.S. was relatively short compared to the time I spent getting there. All of the divine encounters along the way were God-ordained.

After I left Oregon and continued north, my GPS led me to back roads which brought me to the beautiful "Tunnel of Trees." I marveled at the massive height and majesty of these gorgeous trees. This road and the surrounding trees reminded me of the straight and narrow path to heaven. In Matthew 7:13 - 14 Jesus tells us, "Enter through the narrow gate. For wide is the gate and broad is the road that leads to destruction, and many enter through it. But small is the gate and narrow the road that leads to life, and only a few find it."

As soon as I exited the Tunnel of Trees, I ended up in Forks, Washington. The name may be familiar to you; it's the actual town where author Stephenie Meyer based her Twilight saga novels. I also read that Forks is the rainiest town in the contiguous United States. That being said, it was

95

dark and rainy, and I was as cold as I've ever been in my life. I stopped at a gas station and had trouble dismounting from my bike. My legs were that stiff and frozen. I went into the restroom and tried to warm myself. I then resorted to standing by the hot food section of the convenience store; anything to get warm!

The women who worked at this gas station/convenience store looked at me and thought that I had lost my mind. They had to be thinking, "Why would someone be riding a motorcycle in this weather?" I approached them and asked where I could find the closest, cheapest room for the night. It turns out that there was a motel near the gas station. I went a short distance and thankfully secured a room. I had a great shower and used the motel hairdryer on my boots and gloves. They were wet and cold so I kept the dryer on them for a while. Everything was dry in the morning, all praise to God!

Looking back, God once again protected me and brought me through the storm. I did some laundry in the morning and was on my way to Neah Bay, Washington, my second corner!

I did not spend a lot of time in Neah Bay. I took some pictures and the Lord brought a man across my path who I talked to about the Lord. I checked Bunk-A-Biker which led me to Jeff and Eric in Grayland, Washington. These brothers gave me a nice place to stay at their house. I hung out with Jeff who gave me a tour of the area the next day. After a great day in Grayland, I headed back to California via the beautiful Pacific Coast Highway. I was on the way to the third corner of my journey.

THE THIRD
CORNER

BACK TO CALIFORNIA

My second time in California was relatively short as I headed to the San Diego—Mexico border which would be my third corner. I was in awe of all God had done, thinking about how He brought me from Pennsylvania, to Maine, to the tip of Washington state, and now back to California. My needs had not only been met, but abundantly exceeded beyond belief. I'd met some amazing people and I believe God allowed me to be a blessing to them, and they had also been a blessing to me. I survived weather events and several setbacks. And my bike was still going strong! He allowed me to take this journey, not only telling people about Jesus but also allowing me to do what I love to do – ride my bike and enjoy His creation. He proved Psalm 37:4 true before my very eyes: "Take delight in the Lord, and he will give you the desires of your heart."

Several wonderful people provided places to stay in California through the Bunk-A-Biker site. Greg and Kelley provided the use of their RV for my first night back in

California. They fed and blessed me as I made my way south.

While I continued along the Pacific Coast Highway, I would typically stop at various scenic overlooks to take in the beautiful views. Each stop did not disappoint as I stood in awe of the spectacular scenery that God created.

At one of the stops, a man named Jonathan pulled up on his bike. It amazes me how the Lord can bring people together in spite of their differences. Jonathan has much different views than I do politically but we became friends. We rode together for a while and I enjoyed every minute of the experience. I like to keep it "real" so I'll confess that we were flying down the mountain and it was so enjoyable. Doing what I love and taking in the beauty of His creation are the things that bring me great joy! Later on, Jonathan sent me a video of our ride, put to Christian music. It's a keepsake for this memorable encounter orchestrated by God. Check it out at: https://tinyurl.com/JR-JonathanPCH

Bunk-A-Biker led me to stay with Ann and Becky who were wonderful ladies in Clearlake, California. They provided me with supper and a good night's sleep. After that, Karen and Scott provided shelter for the night in Novato, California. I'm not particularly fond of cats but their little kitten jumped up on my shoulders and we made friends. Karen and Scott provided meals and hospitality. Karen and I went for a ride on some twisty, curvy roads. She is a skilled rider and took the turns pretty quickly. With the load on my bike, I was scraping my floorboards trying to keep up with her!

I loved the San Diego area and the great weather. The evening before Thanksgiving, I decided to enjoy the outdoors, so I pulled my bike under a palm tree, unpacked my sleeping bag, and slept under the stars. What a peaceful night in the gorgeous weather, being still before my Lord.

When I worked as a mechanic back home, I had two loyal customers, Rose and Gerry. I am so thankful that a number of customers I saw at the shop are also friends of mine. Prior to embarking on my journey, Rose and Gerry asked for my phone number so that they could follow my progress and check in on me.

It was the day before Thanksgiving as I made my way closer to the third corner of the U.S. when Rose got ahold of me and asked, "Jimmy, is there any chance that you will be in San Diego tomorrow, Thanksgiving Day?" I said, "Yes, I'm actually headed there right now." Rose and Gerry's daughter, Andrea, and her husband, Will, along with their children wanted to invite me to their home for Thanksgiving. Will has served our country in the Marine Corps for more than 30 years now.

I went to a park where I planned to meet up with Andrea. I met an off-duty police officer there which turned out to be another divine appointment. I told the officer about my journey and he offered to pray for my daughter, Heavyn. It was such a blessing and I am grateful for this encounter. And once again I was amazed at the connections God makes in our lives and how He brought yet another divine encounter across my path.

I had texted Andrea to arrange our meeting at the park. She sent me her address where I met up with her and her family. We had some great food and wonderful conversation. Before I left, Andrea handed me some money and said, "This is from Mom and Dad." This was another example of God's abundant provision.

I made my way to Silver Strand State Beach on Coronado Island. This was an unintended stop, but yet another one which God had ordained. I met Daniel and Jenna and talked to them about Jesus and my journey. We were enjoying great conversation and they asked me if I would stay a while and hang out with them at the beach. I learned on this journey to write my plans in pencil and give God the eraser. So when He set up an appointment, I went with His plans. I hung out at the beach with them and we talked about Jesus. I enjoyed a gorgeous sunset before departing. Daniel and Jenna prayed with me before I left.

The next morning, I had made it to the third corner: the California–Mexico border. After spending some time at the border, it was time to leave California and head towards my fourth corner. But God had lots for me to do before that.

HOW CAN I SAY "GOODBYE" IF YOU WON'T LET ME LEAVE?

Here I was on my way to Arizona and New Mexico, thankful and amazed that my bike was still going! I'd survived an unexplainable clutch problem in Ohio, the clutch and voltage regulator failures in California, God's protection through ice, snow, and rain, and minimal service
102

for my bike (oil change, new back tire, new rear brake pads). But reality set in before I could get out of California. My bike started acting up, so I got off of the interstate. I was tired and it was late so I found a spot in a parking lot and retired to my sleeping bag for the night.

The next morning, I entered a gas station and asked where I could find help. I could not continue my journey until the bike was fixed. The store clerk directed me to a big truck shop down the road. The bike was still cutting out but I was able to make it to the shop. I met a wonderful man named Pablo, the owner of the garage, who took a look at my bike. We played around with the electrical connections and checked the fuses. Our thought was that perhaps there was a loose wire. We applied some grease to the electrical connections which appeared to do the trick; the bike was back in business and running fine. Pablo graciously treated me to an authentic Mexican breakfast which was great!

As I drove away from the shop, I sensed the Lord speaking to me as He had done so often. For some reason, He was calling me to go back. I no sooner pulled into the lot when a man named Javier walked over to meet me. He started the conversation by talking about how impressed he was with the "stuff" on my bike. But it became clear that there was something deeper going on. Javier was going through some problems in his marriage. I am no expert but can certainly sympathize given my own experiences. Javier said, "I felt like I needed to talk to you." I knew once again that this was all God's doing! We talked and cried together. I prayed for Javier before I left. You've heard me say it before but this was yet another divine appointment that only God can arrange.

I continued east, but it wasn't long before my bike started to have issues again. The ground wire between the battery and the frame had come apart. I pulled into an auto parts store for help. A kind lady employed at the store was a great help. She helped me fabricate another ground cable. A mechanic from a garage next door to the shop loaned me tools so that I could make the fix. This is significant because mechanics are typically protective of their tools and do not loan them to strangers. But when God is in something, amazing things happen! The auto store clerk would not take any money when I asked for the cost of the parts. She said, "I love what you're doing." And I had opportunity to share Jesus with her. My bike was running great and it was off to Arizona and New Mexico.

Can God use mechanical issues with a motorcycle to touch people's lives? I think you know the answer!

THE LAND OF ENCHANTMENT

I made my way out of Arizona and entered the state of New Mexico. I had not anticipated any bad weather, but a digital highway billboard indicated danger ahead: Snow and ice. It was freezing cold and I noticed the buildup of snow and ice on both sides of the interstate. "Lord, what should I do?" I sensed Him saying, "Keep going." I knew that He would protect me as He had on this entire journey.

I was in the middle of nowhere and the light on my fuel gauge told me that I needed gas, very soon. Thankfully I came to a gas station but it was closed due to the pandemic.

I thought that I would be stuck in New Mexico, in the desert. Maybe this would be the first time I had to set up my tent?

I don't understand how (well, actually I do, it was all God!) but suddenly I entered the town I was headed to. And there was a gas station, open for business! I met a man who drove a cool looking Rock Crawler truck. He handed me some money and bought lunch for me. It was a double-blessing to find gas when I did and to meet this generous man.

You'll recall that my landlords, Don and Teresa, generously took care of my rent and affairs at home while I was away. It is not an understatement to say that my journey would not have been possible without them. Before I left Pennsylvania to begin the journey, they asked me for one thing: A couple from their church had moved to New Mexico to start a prison ministry. Don and Teresa asked that I look this couple up when I got to the state. "Please stop by their house, tell them we love them, and tell them about your journey." I asked them to write down the name, address, and phone number of the people I was to visit. I recognized "Brian's" name and asked a few questions about him. It turns out that Brian was a friend from high school and we had graduated together. Once again, God astounded me with these divine appointments!

So, this was the main reason I planned to stop in New Mexico: to fulfill the request of my landlords. It was the least I could after all they were doing for me.

I arrived at the address my landlords had given me but no one was home. I waited outside the house for at least an hour and it was cold. Finally, a neighbor named "Anthony" came over. I greeted him and asked, "Do you know who lives here and when they'll be home?" I learned that I was at the right house but Anthony did not know when Brian and Rochelle would return. Anthony invited me into his home and left phone messages for both Brian and Rochelle. Anthony and I sat together for the better part of three hours, talking about Jesus.

Rochelle called Anthony back and we learned that Brian was away on a hunting trip and would not return until Monday. Anthony asked where I was staying. I hadn't thought that far ahead so he insisted on taking care of my accommodations. He said, "You've blessed me tonight so I want to bless you." I replied, "If you find me the cheapest place in town, I'll go." It turned out to be a very nice place, I'm sure not very cheap. In fact, the next day Rochelle asked me where I had stayed. When I told her, she informed me that the hotel I stayed in was the nicest in town! Anthony had been generous, displaying the love of Jesus. I take no credit and give all glory to God, but Anthony told me that my visit led him closer to the Lord. He was struggling but he is getting his life back together. I praise God for this!

Since Brian would not be home until Monday, I made the best use of my time while in town. I messaged Rochelle and asked if I could come to her church on Sunday. When I entered the church, the pastor took notice and came over to me. It was cold outside, and from the way I was dressed, obvious that I came on a bike. The pastor greeted me and said, "Are you on a motorcycle?" I responded that I was, and that I was also friends with Brian. Pastor Larry said, "Wait until you hear my message!" Hmm, I wondered what was in store.

The pastor preached about how Paul traveled to different places, spreading the Gospel. Paul did not have the benefit of a motorcycle but I saw the parallel between our journeys. Interestingly, when the pastor finished preaching, he said, "I'm done talking, do any of you have any questions or comments?" I felt the Holy Spirit telling me to go forward but argued that it wasn't a good idea because I wasn't a member of the congregation. I was a stranger and didn't want to take attention away from the pastor's message. But there was that voice again from God. "Jimmy, go ahead up and tell them about your journey." I argued but God kept pressing it on my heart to go forward. I prayed, "Lord, if You want me to go up there, You need to make it happen." I had barely finished my prayer when Pastor Larry stopped mid-sentence and went "radio silent." He stopped talking and turned his head towards me. "Jimmy, would you like to come up and share what you're doing with us?"

I have no words to describe how awesome God is. He made it happen even though I argued and pretty much put the burden on Him. He is good, all the time! I was able to share my journey with this congregation. As I went to leave, two different men stopped me and shook my hand. When they walked away my hand was holding money that they had placed there. Once again, God was providing for me on this journey.

The blessings were far from finished. Pastor Larry approached and said, "Follow me, I got you a room for a couple nights until Brian gets home." I was so grateful. The hotel room was for sleeping; I rode around the area and told as many people as I could about Jesus. Gas stations were my greatest source for opportunities to talk to people. This was true from the time I left Pennsylvania until I returned there many months later.

The next morning the phone in my hotel room rang. The front desk told me that a gentleman had left an envelope for me. When I went to the front desk, I retrieved the envelope. The church had blessed me with a generous donation. I then helped two women carry bags to their respective rooms. They insisted on giving me money even though I protested. However, they said they wanted to bless me so I could not deny them. I spoke to a number of employees there whom God led me to talk to. One woman told me that she was struggling with some issues. I just listened and we cried together. God continued to move as I waited for my friend to return from his hunting trip.

On Monday, I learned that Brian had come home. Somehow Rochelle and everyone else kept it a secret that I was in town. When I knocked on the door, Rochelle answered and called to her husband, "Brian, there is someone here to see you!" What a great reunion it was. He was so surprised to see me! I told him about how my wonderful landlords had arranged this meeting and what I was doing on this journey.

Brian took me to the Transition Home for inmates where he works. He and his friend Byron, a former inmate, had started this ministry called "Byron's House of Hope." Byron had a vision to help former prisoners assimilate back into society. Both men have a compassion for former inmates and it shows. Sadly, Byron is no longer with us but his dream lives on.

I was blessed with the opportunity to speak to the people and share my testimony. I don't know what God has in store for me going forward but I share my friends' passion for the ministry and these people. I remember my own experience when I was released from prison, and the need to learn life skills and fit back into society.

Brian showed me around the area and we spent precious time together, talking about the Lord and catching up on old times. He took me to a place called "Angel Peak" which reminded me of a mini-Grand Canyon. Brian suggested that we make a Facebook live video to capture the moment and we did that. I was invited to speak at a church in town which Brian was familiar with. I shared my journey and testimony, and the Pastor blessed me with a financial gift for my journey. Check out the Facebook video at https://tinyurl.com/JR-UndefinedWasLive

While the blessings were many in New Mexico, not every encounter with people was positive. One evening, I was stopped at a traffic light and four men tried to jump me. God protected me as I was able to quickly slip away on my bike. He was not done with me on my journey.

I spent the better part of five days in New Mexico, the Land of Enchantment. The time with Brian, Rochelle, Anthony, Pastor Larry, and many others I met there was memorable. As I made my way towards Texas, I noticed two billboards on the interstate. On the right billboard was the statement, "Jesus is watching over you." On the left billboard was an advertisement for an adult bookstore. This reminded me that we are to be lights for Jesus in a very dark world.

MAKING MY WAY TO THE
SUNSHINE STATE

When I went through Texas the first time, on my way to Washington state, I was just passing through at the top of the state. I had taken a more southern route across the U.S. to the west coast to avoid winter weather (which I did – mostly). This time was different. I was on a very southern route now and God had some divine appointments set up for me. I would spend several days in the Lone Star State.

While I was making my way through Texas, my Aunt Connie sent me a message reminding me that our former pastor from Pennsylvania had a church in the Houston area. The message read, "Why don't you stop by and say hi?" I did an internet search and discovered that Pastor John's church was on the way to my fourth corner, Key West, Florida. This route would take me right by the church!

I stopped for gas and thought about getting a room for the night. It was pouring rain and I wanted to find a place to stay and start out fresh in the morning. I asked the Lord to confirm my plans and His voice told me to keep riding to the church. It was late Saturday night when I arrived at Pastor John's church. The building was dark and it was still raining heavily. I started to set up camp in a gazebo but there was no protection from the rain there. I rode my bike up a sidewalk to a doorway, in a recessed area of the building, which would provide protection for me and the bike. I opened up my sleeping bag and fell asleep on the concrete sidewalk.

I was in a sound sleep when a voice woke me up the next morning. "Sir, are you okay"? Tony and Paul from the church's music ministry had arrived to set up for their Sunday worship services. We exchanged greetings and they handed me a breakfast burrito. "Are you coming back for the service?" they asked. I told them that I would return.

I drove to a local Waffle House for breakfast where I met my server, Kathelyn. This was another divine appointment. We talked for the better part of an hour about the Lord and the journey I was on. After a good breakfast I rode back to the church for the worship service.

I was standing in the back of the church and noticed Pastor John heading for the pulpit. I walked towards him and he spotted me. "Jimmy, what are you doing in Texas?" He was surprised to see me there but I was amazed and grateful that he remembered me; I had not seen him in several years. I shared a brief summary of my journey but he needed to start the service. Pastor John said, "Here, take

112

my number and send me yours; we'll get together later today." I was so blessed by the first service that I stayed for the second!

After church I did what I love to do: I rode around seeking people to talk to about Jesus. I sensed God's voice instructing me to talk to a nearby police officer. I am amazed at the number of law enforcement officers the Lord brought across my path during the journey! I rode up and asked the kind officer if there was a local park where I could talk to people about the Lord and my journey. He gave me directions to a park, which was close by.

I arrived at the park and sat down on a bench, wondering who God would send to me. It wasn't long before a man named Mark approached me after noticing my bike. Like many others on my journey, he was curious about what I was doing and asked several questions. I felt led to tell him about my past, including my time with the KKK. God had transformed my heart and now I had a passion for all people. I shared with Mark about the missions trips I had taken to the country of Haiti.

Mark left and went back to his car. After a short time, he returned and said, "I want to show you something." Mark shared some writing he had created on his phone expressing hatred for a specific people group. I was shocked at the tone of the words; it was nasty, racist stuff. He said to me, "Because of your testimony and what you shared with me, I'm deleting this from my phone. I don't want to be a racist anymore. I want a relationship with God. My friends, I take no credit for this radical change in Mark's heart. It's all God's doing!

113

While I was talking to Mark, two teenage girls had walked by to the other side of a large pond which was a part of the park. They sensed God telling them to speak with me so they turned around and walked back to join me at the park bench. The girls' names are Adrienne and Emily. Emily only stayed for a short time because she had to go to work. Adrienne hung around and we talked for a while. Before leaving, she asked if she could pray for me and I agreed, only if I could pray for her. We had a meaningful time of prayer together and Adrienne asked if I would attend her church that same evening. I said that I would and looked forward to the service.

As I walked around the lake, I noticed a snake making its way towards the water. It was early December so I thought it unusual to see a snake at that time of year. But this was Texas, not Pennsylvania! I tried to catch the snake but he slithered into the water before I could get to him. Did I tell you that I love snakes?

That evening I went to Emily and Adrienne's church as promised. I was blessed by the worship and message but did not see the ladies until the service was over. Adrienne had purchased a large jar of peanuts for me to take along on my journey. She pointed out that they were "unsalted;" she was looking out for my health!

Pastor John had asked that I come to his house at 8 p.m. so I headed there after church. His wife Amy made a delicious supper consisting of beef, mashed potatoes, and carrots, and I was so grateful. John and Amy really took care of me that night! We spoke for hours, talking about everything from Jason to my journey and we had a great

114

time catching up. They showed me my room and I had a nice shower. I spent the night in their comfortable guest room with a beautiful bed. I had a great night's sleep and was so thankful to reconnect with a pastor who had done so much for me in my walk with Jesus Christ.

The following morning Pastor John treated me to breakfast where we had a great time of fellowship. After we prayed together, John left. A man named Randy pulled up into the parking lot for breakfast when he noticed my bike. He was curious, so he came up to me and asked what I was doing. I told him about my journey and he gave me a donation for gas. Once again God had provided abundantly!

I was back on the road when Dianna contacted me. Recall that I met her and Majorie at the Canada gas station in Arizona, on the way to my second corner. Dianna actually lives in Texas but was visiting Arizona when I was on my way to the West Coast. Dianna had been following my journey on social media and knew that I was in Texas, making my way towards Florida. She asked if I would be willing to stop by her house and talk to her grandchildren about my journey. Even though her house would take me miles off of my planned route, how could I say no? I saw every invitation as a divine appointment. It's the reason I was on this journey. So, I got directions and headed to Dianna's home.

I arrived at Dianna's and we greeted each other. I met her husband Mike and their grandkids. Then they called their neighbors, Cody and Jenny, who came over to the house. We sat around and talked about my journey.

115

Cody was struggling with some things and brought to tears by our conversation. The grandkids listened intently which really impressed me. They were focused on everything said by the adults! Cody gave me a metal cross which is engraved with his and Dianna's family names along with the date of my visit. This cross sits on top of the wooden one, displayed on my bike. He also gave me a camouflage backpack which I use to store all of my food and drinks when I ride. Mike gave me a donation to allow me to continue on my journey.

Before I left Texas I met "Ariel" who is a mounted police officer. She was on duty, on her horse, and I was able to share my journey with her. I also ate at a restaurant called "Spanky's." When I saw the name of the establishment, I knew that I had to stop and eat there. I wanted to mention this in the book because my Uncle Don gave me the name "Spanky" when I was a child.

PELICANS AND MAGNOLIA

My bike was pointed east and I did not plan for any significant stops between Texas and Florida. Still, no matter where I went on this journey, the Lord had people for me to meet. Sometimes I stayed for a while, and other times, the encounters were brief. Either way, my heart and ears were open to the divine appointments He set up. I made a few brief stops in Louisiana and Mississippi before entering Florida.

Louisiana's nickname is "The Pelican State," evidently because there are many pelicans along the Gulf of

Mexico and Mississippi River. I also learned that the Pelican is displayed on the Louisiana flag. Even though my time there was short, God was clearly at work.

I stopped for a bite to eat at a place called the "Rice Palace." I was able to share my story with my server, Ashley, and a police officer named, "Gilbert." He was a believer and gave me some Jesus fish-emblem necklaces to give to people I met. I handed every one of those out on my journey except for one I kept for myself; it is displayed proudly in my kitchen now!

At the Cajun Harley dealership, I spoke to Wayne, Hannah, and Tatum about my journey. I also added a sticker from the shop to my bike. Later, at Gator's gas station, I met an employee named Robin who worked in the convenience store. We talked about everything from snakes to Jesus. I had never had boiled peanuts, so Robin gave me some for free. We talked for hours. As we spoke, I learned that Robin worked by herself and was concerned about her safety when she was alone in the store at night. I felt led to stay with her for several hours to ensure that she was safe. I left a little before closing time, convinced that God had me there to protect her.

As I entered Mississippi, the Lord led me to a small hotel where I met Michelle, who worked at the front desk. I understand that Mississippi's nickname is the "Magnolia State," evidently due to its beautiful Magnolia trees. After talking about my journey, Michelle gave me a discounted room which I greatly appreciated. I was able to share my journey with a motel maid and a nice man who only had one leg. I was blessed by his positive outlook on life, despite his

117

physical limitations. It reminded me of how much we can take for granted. It was a great stay with more divine appointments and provisions from the Lord.

On my way to Florida, Spur told me to call a man named "Moe" who was part of the Hellfighter's Motorcycle Ministry. I called, and Moe asked if I would be willing to come and speak at the Living Room, the Hellfighter's ministry clubhouse in Pensacola, Florida. Of course, I agreed, recognizing this as yet another divine appointment from God.

MY TEMPORARY HOME IN FLORIDA

I never intended to stay in Florida for four-and-a-half months, but I was there from December of 2020 until April of 2021. So much happened while I was in the Sunshine State, including a few trials.

I've said this a few times and will probably say it again because it is one of the main reasons I wrote this book: You can't look at my journey and not see God all through it. God provided for me the entire time!

My plan was to ride through Florida, hit the fourth corner in Key West, and then head home. But God had other plans which Spur had made clear when he said to me, "Our Heavenly Father told me that you'd be spending the winter in Florida." That was not what I wanted to hear, nor what I intended to do. But I learned that His ways are much better than what I could ever come up with. I have seen it proven over and over again, so all I could do was trust Him!

I planned to arrive in town by midweek. I asked Moe if there were any abandoned houses or sheds where I could stay in the Pensacola area. He said he would check and get back to me. He sent me the address of a motel where I could stay for a few nights before I would speak on Saturday evening. The Hellfighter's graciously put me up at the motel for several days.

I arrived in town and checked in to the motel. Moe expressed his concern about my accommodations and asked, "Is this motel good enough for you?" It was more than good enough; I had slept on the ground many times on the journey, but even that was a blessing because God provided warm nights to sleep outdoors!

I rode around town talking to anyone I could. I found Pensacola Harley and met a number of people there including Nik, Mary, Spencer, Steven, Lee, DeWayne, William, Kurt, and others. I shared my story and why I was on this journey. I met so many people around town.

That Saturday I made a short trip across the border to Alabama to check out a marina which was recommended to me. It was a cool site to see but there was no one to talk to. My GPS took me back to Florida on an unfamiliar route and it had started to rain. I was doing between 45-50 miles-per-hour when I crossed through an intersection. To my horror, without signage or warning, the road turned from blacktop to muddy red clay.

I fully expected to go down as my bike started "dancing." I was out of control, slipping and sliding as mud several inches deep had caked onto my tires. I didn't have time for a lengthy prayer so just cried out, "Lord help me!" What happened next defied the laws of physics and was nothing short of miraculous. My bike stood straight up and I regained complete control of it. A vehicle with front-wheel drive was heading towards me and the driver was struggling to maintain control. I can't imagine what she must have been thinking as I passed by, riding like I was on dry blacktop. I thought, "Jesus, I'm so glad that You know how to ride a Harley!" God had miraculously protected me once again and reminded me that He is interested in even the smallest details of our lives.

The Living Room clubhouse was built in, what I would consider, a dangerous part of town. This was by design as the club's desire is to minister to the community. And it's obvious that God was drawing people from all walks of life to this ministry. My understanding is that the building was originally the Dixie Restaurant which was a "whites-only" establishment in the 1940s-1950s. And now here I was, enabled by God to speak here. Everyone is welcome at their Saturday night service which warmed my heart. I met some great brothers at the club including Moe, Cyclone, Tomahawk, George, David, Fonz, Bulldog, Hillbilly, and others. It was a great blessing and privilege to speak at the Living Room that Saturday evening. When I was done the ministry gave me a generous donation.

The Hellfighter's have a passion to fulfill the Great Commission, going into the world, preaching the Gospel and making disciples. Each member has a matching tattoo

121

in the shape of a cross which reads "ETW" diagonally and vertically. The acronym stands for, "End Time Warriors, Evangelizing the World." It's a tangible reminder of their mission.

Cyclone invited me to his house for their Sunday School class Christmas party. I enjoyed a wonderful meal with him, his wife Angel, their son Alex, daughter Raegan, and members of their class. As I was leaving, we all held hands and they prayed for me. I always appreciated the prayers of brothers and sisters in Christ. During the prayer, Raegan let go of my hand and hugged me with her head on my side. As I bundled up to go, Raegan gave me a big hug and said, "Come back soon." That little girl holds a special place in my heart.

I met Haley and her husband Roman on a stop at Brown's Grocery which is part gas station and part convenience store in Holt, Florida. Haley asked about my "Broken Chain's" sweatshirt. Her shoulder was hurting so I asked if I could pray for her to be healed. I had the opportunity to share my testimony and journey with her and Roman as they were eating. They were amazed at what God had been doing on my trip around the country. When we finished talking and I was ready to leave, they gave me a donation for my journey.

I had been looking to get my bike serviced again when I first got to Florida. With all of the miles I had accumulated it was time for another oil change and regular maintenance. Moe had given me the name of a guy, but he was away for a few days and we wouldn't be able to connect. So, the maintenance would have to wait.

"TINY"

I didn't understand it, but for some reason God was telling me to call a man named "Tiny." Spur had given me Tiny's name earlier to possibly service my bike, but Moe got ahold of me first. Now God was laying Tiny on my heart. Tiny lives in Pensacola and I was already an hour past there, heading in the direction of Key West. It didn't make sense to go back, but God's voice persisted. I didn't know Tiny and he didn't know me. If I called, what would I say?

God had always blessed my obedience on this journey, so I called Tiny. Tiny never answers his phone at work but for some reason (another God-ordained miracle), he picked up when I called. When he answered, I introduced myself. "I'm not sure why I'm calling but I felt God telling me to contact you." Tiny replied, "I wanted to meet you. Did you ever get your bike serviced?" I told Tiny that the original plan didn't work out. Tiny replied, "Be at my house at 5:30 tonight, I'll service your bike."

Tiny sent me his address and asked what type of bike I was riding. I found out that he stopped after work and purchased all of the parts he would need for the maintenance on my bike. When I arrived at the house, Tiny's garage door was open and he was ready to work. We talked about Jesus while he diligently performed the needed maintenance on my Harley.

Tiny would not take a dime for the parts and all of his hard labor. As a matter of fact, he said, "It's getting late, you're staying here with me." Tiny fried up a hefty amount of fish, hush puppies, and fries. There was a ton of leftovers when we were finished eating.

I asked Tiny why he had cooked so much food. His reply was, "That is what I felt led to do." Tiny helped me with my laundry in the morning but his dryer would not work. He tried running it twice but the machine never dried the clothes. The dryer had never done this before (or since) and I believe it was because the Lord wanted us to spend more time together. We spent the entire day together and he said, "Tonight I'll introduce you to some people."

Along with the divine appointments God was arranging, He also provided many wonderful opportunities to visit beautiful sites and to learn new things. Tiny asked his neighbor, Tom, if he could take us on a tour of a nearby military base and museum. Tom is a retired Army special forces drill sergeant and accompanied us to the base. We spent hours there, taking in the history of the facility. I had a great time and was impressed with everything I saw!

Tiny and I went out for supper at a restaurant named "McGuire's." This place has dollar bills hanging from the walls and ceilings. I'm told that the value of the bills is over $2 million and they were quite the sight to see! The cost of dinner was sizeable, but Tiny treated, and I was grateful. There, I also met Heather, who works at the restaurant, and shared my story with her. She was brought to tears and hugged me before I left. Heather wanted to hear more about my journey so we met for breakfast a few days later where we talked some more. After Heather and I had breakfast, I met William, a homeless man, and shared my journey. He prayed for me and I prayed for him before heading back to Tiny's.

Tiny invited me to go along to the Outlaw's clubhouse. I was concerned because Tiny's girlfriend and another friend said, "You can't take him there on church night. Tiny took me anyway. As we entered the clubhouse Tiny announced, "Hey everybody, this is Jimmy, he's with the FBI." I was a little anxious because every eye was on me. I asked the Lord what I should do and I sensed Him saying, "Give it back." So, I responded, "Tiny how many times do I have to tell you, I got no problem whooping you and praying for a healing when I'm done." Everyone had a laugh and a calm fell over the room.

Tiny told his fellow members that I was a motorcycle evangelist, riding around the country telling people about Jesus. He then said, "I thought you guys might want to hear what he has to say." One man loudly stated, "Did you come here to save us?" I replied, "I can't save you but I can lead you to the One who can." We all had a great time talking about Jesus in the clubhouse.

It was mid-December when Tiny and I went to visit his friends Robby and Jacqueline. Robby is a mentor to Tiny and we spoke for a while about my journey. I was so touched when Robby prayed about a phone call I planned to make the following day to my daughter, Heavyn. I wasn't sure that she would talk to me because she never answered when I called in the past. Robby prayed, specifically, that she would answer and that we would have a conversation. God miraculously answered Robby's prayer as I spoke with Heavyn the next day. Robby and Jacqueline gave a gift of soft blankets to Tiny and me as we left.

I talked Tiny into going to Robby's church with me on Sunday. It was a great service and to my blessing I got to witness Tiny go forward for the altar call.

In total, I spent the better part of a week with Tiny. God had amazed me once again because the leftovers from Tiny's fish fry provided my food for the week. As far as he was concerned, his house was my house. Tiny became a great friend and remains a close brother to this day.

It was time to head to my fourth corner, Key West.

Me and Tiny

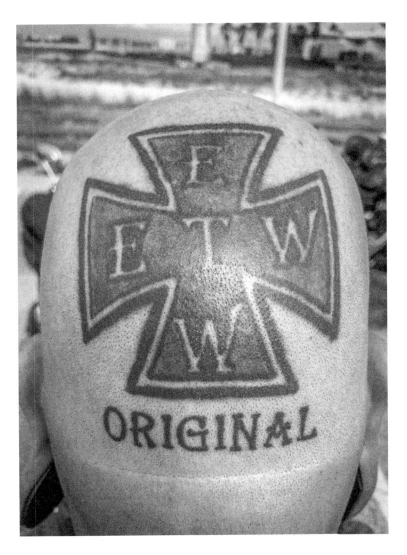

The ETW Symbol

THE FOURTH CORNER

THE SOUTHERNMOST POINT

At this time, I was still in the panhandle of Florida. My goal was to make it to Key West by Christmas. I found Tony and his wife Hippie through Bunk-A-Biker and spent a night at their place. This nice couple gave me use of their motorhome which was parked in the backyard. They have a heart for people as they provide campground-type spaces and hookups for travelers. I met Eddie and his wife Debbie who were there in their motorhome. We all sat and talked around a fire about my journey. I remain friends with these fine people to this day. Tony and Hippie asked if I would speak at their New Year's Eve church service on my way back from Key West. Of course, I agreed to do that.

My aunt contacted me and told me about some friends who lived in North Port, Florida, just below Tampa. I called her friends, Mike and Cindy, who offered to put me up for a night. My aunt had told them about my journey and they were eager to help me out. I called them and made my way to their home. The couple fed me dinner and provided a nice room for the night, and breakfast in the morning. I saw my first alligator (in their front yard) and visited "Dog Beach."

When I left their place, I was on the road all day heading south. At some point, Spur called and told me that he had arranged for me to speak at an Alcoholics Anonymous/Narcotics Anonymous (AA/NA) meeting. A man named "Cutter" was my contact person. I arrived early to make sure I was at the right place. When I got there, a meeting was already in progress. I was invited in for dinner which I really appreciated. Shortly after that, it was time for the 8:30 meeting where I had the opportunity to share my testimony. I met a number of great people and was blessed to share what God has done in my life. When the meeting was over Cutter took me to his place to stay for the night.

After crossing the scenic Seven Mile Bridge, I had finally arrived in the Florida Keys. Admiring the surrounding seas, I thought about how much I would love to go out on a boat and fish in the ocean. I checked around and learned that the cost to take such a fishing trip was expensive. I spoke to the Father and said, "Lord, if you want me to go, You'll make it happen." I purchased two hot dogs at a convenience store and prayed before my meal. While I was praying, I sensed someone close to me. A man named Corey had been sitting in his SUV and walked over to me. He said, "I saw you praying, are you a Christian? While I was sitting here, God told me to walk over and take you fishing." Corey handed me his business card and told me that he was a fishing guide. I appreciated the gesture but told Corey that I couldn't afford to go. Corey said, "You don't understand, God wants me to take you fishing, it won't cost

132

you anything." This was an answer to my prayers, but I needed to pause before accepting the offer. I sincerely believed I was to get to my fourth corner by Christmas, and moving forward was the only way to accomplish that. Corey offered to take me fishing in the future, so I knew I could graciously accept if the opportunity aligned then, but for now I needed to get back on the road. I was just grateful to see God work again in a way that truly could have only been Him. He was constantly reassuring me that He would provide not only for my needs, but also for the desires of my heart.

KEY WEST, FLORIDA

At 4 p.m. on Christmas day, December 25th, 2020, I arrived at my destination, the southernmost city in the contiguous United States. If you've ever been to Key West, you know that it's the "law" that you visit and have your picture taken at the Southernmost Point Buoy. I'm joking about this actually being law but this tourist attraction is one of the most visited and photographed attractions in the United States. Most people who visit Key West have their picture taken here. I did things a little differently as I rode my bike up the sidewalk and had my picture taken right next to the buoy!

I had reached my fourth corner and reflected on the miles I had put on my bike to get here. As usual the Lord brought people across my path, including Keith, Rebecca and Derek. I shared my story with them and we became friends.

After I left the Southernmost Point marker I drove around and came up to a stop sign. I noticed a homeless couple sitting on the side of the road and my heart was burdened for them. I greeted them with a short, "How are you?" I learned that David and his wife, Samantha, were down and out. It was Christmas, they were homeless, hungry, and had no place to stay. I sensed God telling me to "feed them." I hesitated for a moment. After all, I didn't have a lot of money. I heard God saying, "It's my money, I'll give you more. Feed them!" It was indeed God's money. He had provided everything I needed, and then some, for my entire journey. So, I bought this couple dinner with God's money.

After the meal at a food trailer, we retreated back to the spot where we had met. I offered to pray for David and Samantha and asked about their specific needs. Based on what they told me, I prayed that David would find work to support his family. At the exact time I was praying for a job for David, I heard his phone "ding."

When we were done praying, David picked up his phone to check the message which had just come in, and he began to cry. A man had texted to let David know that he had been hired for a new job and would start at 8 a.m. the next morning. Once again, God had answered my prayers and left me in awe of His goodness! The following day, Samantha posted this on social media: "We were down but God sent us an angel on a Harley." She said that this was the best Christmas they had experienced in a long time. As I think about it now, it was one of the best Christmases I ever had as well. I was alone on Christmas day and God chose to bless me with this divine encounter.

I was close to the aquarium in Key West when a pastor from Texas named Troy approached me. Troy travels all over to rescue people victimized by human trafficking. We talked about my journey and he invited me to dinner, but I didn't want to be a third wheel. He offered to put me up for the night, which I really appreciated, but I wouldn't let him; the prices in Key West are much too expensive. He then said, "If you ever need a room, wherever you are in the country, just call me." He gave me a generous donation and we still keep in contact. I would love to get back to Texas and visit his church. This was yet another divine appointment.

Near the aquarium I had pulled my bike up and found a great spot to set up my sleeping bag next to the building. The next morning, I woke up and asked the Lord what I should do next. I sensed Him saying, "Be still." I took this as confirmation for what Spur had told me, that our Heavenly Father said I would be staying in Florida for the Winter.

Shortly after that I was surprised to receive a message from Samantha. She asked, "Did you find a good place to sleep last night?" I told her that I had settled next to the aquarium. Incredibly, she and David were right near the aquarium ticket booth. We had spent the night literally feet from one another. It was another "coincidence" that only God can set up. I bought breakfast and coffee for Samantha because David was off to start his first day of work.

A friendly groundskeeper named Jeff came over and told me that I could spend about 30 more minutes in my spot, before he needed to operate his leaf blower. It was time to get up anyway so I spoke with Jeff for a few minutes. He gave me a gift card to Starbucks which blessed me.

I met so many wonderful people in Key West. I ran into Noah and Liam who were searching for their stolen bicycle. They had looked everywhere to find it but to no avail. I shared my journey with them and then, miraculously, they located their bike in a place where they had previously looked. They claimed that speaking with me helped them find the bike but all glory goes to God!

As I waited for the coffee shop to open, I met Darla. Like so many on my journey, she noticed my bike and wanted to know more. She graciously bought my coffee and we chatted for a while. I learned that she lives near Sturgis, South Dakota, the place I dreamed about since I was a boy. She said if I ever get to Sturgis to look her up. My dream to visit Sturgis ultimately came true in 2021, on my third journey. I didn't get to connect with Darla at that time, but we still keep in touch.

I left Key West and met up with Corey again in Plantation Key. We never did get to take the fishing trip but we spent two days together, talking about the Lord and sightseeing.

Corey, his friend Michael, and I visited a bird sanctuary. I also stopped to look at a Banyan Tree and was brought to tears by its majesty. This was yet another wonder of God's amazing creation that I got to experience. Corey expressed a desire to join me in ministry but he adheres to a religion which is incompatible with

136

Christianity. We have our differences but we still respect one another.

It was time to head north for an appointment I had promised to keep earlier...

HERE, THERE AND EVERYWHERE IN FLORIDA

I made the long trek back up to the panhandle to speak at Tony and Hippie's church. They put me up in their motor home for a few days and I gave my testimony at the men's breakfast. I went to lunch with a group from Heaven's Way Biker church. A man named "Z" bought everyone's meal and I was thankful for that. Z is a really cool brother. Sadly, Z went home to be with the Lord on March 15, 2021, but I know I'll be reunited with him someday.

I met Reva at the church and saw that she was riding in a Polaris Slingshot. The Slingshot is a three-wheeled motorcycle and I had always wanted to drive one to see what they were like. I gladly accepted when Reva offered to take me for a ride. I jokingly said, "Maybe you'll let me drive on the way back." She said, "We'll see." She did let me drive on the way back and it was a cool experience for me.

God never took a day off on my journey. Chris and Tammy, friends from my home church in Pennsylvania, were on vacation in Florida. They were staying in a rented condo with Chris's mom and dad. They had been following my journey and sent me a message since I would be travelling through their area. The message read, "Would you come by my parent's condo and tell us more about your journey?" As always, I was glad to do it and thankful for the God-ordained opportunity. The visit was a blessing; they bought supper for me and surprised me with a room for the night.

Each night I would post a little diary on my Facebook page, outlining where I was and what God was doing on my journey. I was in the Sarasota area but heading south to experience the Everglades. Brandy, a friend back home, told me that she had a sister in the area so I asked if "she had a shed I could sleep in" and I offered to gladly pay her for a place to stay while I was there. Brandy gave me her sister Darla's number and I called her. Darla and her husband Brett gave me their address and invited me to their home in Cape Coral, Florida. They wanted to hear more of my story. "Coincidentally," Darla remembered me from visits to her sister's home, back in Pennsylvania.

While I was in this area, I wanted to check out a few beaches. At Turtle Beach, I met a woman named Gail. She was sitting on the beach, reading her Bible, when I sensed God telling me to talk with her. We sat and talked for a while. I learned that she has a ministry similar to mine, except that she travels around in her car sharing the Gospel message.

At Siesta Beach, I met a man named Trebor. I was drawn to him when I noticed signs he displayed with the simple messages, "Want prayer? Stop Here" and "America's Only Hope: Jesus Christ." He was evangelizing and giving away small gifts with a Gospel message. He and I talked about my journey when a lady named Shelley approached

138

and asked if she could pray for us. When she finished praying Trebor had to leave, but Shelley and I talked for the better part of thirty minutes. We would have chatted longer but her husband called, asking where she was. She told her husband about my story and then left. But we would connect again...

My friend Lynn from back home knew I was in the area and invited me to dinner with him and his daughter, Anisha. Lynn was in Florida to get his mother settled in at a house she stays in for the winter. Lynn and Anisha took me to Der Dutchman, an Amish restaurant, where I experienced another divine "coincidence." The host sat us in the back of the restaurant and our server was someone I knew from back home, my friend Rachel! She had moved to Florida previously, and now here we were. What are the chances? Rachel was busy so we could only talk for a few minutes, but it was great to reconnect. God had done it once again!

Lynn asked where I planned to stay that night. At that point I had not yet prayed about it so I said, "I don't know." At that very moment, my phone made a noise, indicating that I had a message. Shelley, the woman I met back at Siesta Beach, left me a beautiful message. She expressed her gratitude for our meeting and said that she cried all the way back to her car. She had prayed and asked God to bless someone through her. Shelley said in the message, "I know you need a place to stay tonight so I want to bless you with a room. Here is the address of a hotel. The bill is already taken care of." I was humbled and grateful at what God continued to do through people. Lynn and Anisha were amazed at God's provision! I spent the night at the hotel and enjoyed a good night's sleep. Little did I know that it wouldn't be the only night.

SOMETIMES WE NEED TO "BE STILL" AND SEE WHAT GOD DOES

At the hotel, I woke up the next morning to a severely swollen left foot. I could hardly walk, so I hobbled down to the lobby for the complimentary breakfast. I wasn't sure what I was going to do; I knew that I couldn't ride like this. I gathered my breakfast items and sat down at the table where I prayed over my meal.

As I finished praying, an older gentleman named Andrew at an adjacent table complimented me on my prayer. He was especially impressed at how long I prayed. We spoke for a while about Jesus and my journey. Andrew is a Baptist minister who had travelled there for a speaking engagement in Sarasota. One of his colleagues, Byron, came down for breakfast and joined the conversation. When Andrew had to leave, Byron remained and we spoke for a while longer. Before departing, he handed me some money and prayed for healing of my foot. At the end of his prayer, he surprised me and said, "Can I have that money back?" I said "Sure," not knowing quite what was happening but it was all good. He then said, "As I was sitting here, God told me to give you twice as much instead."

"Now about your foot..." We went to the front desk and Byron asked the clerk if there was a cheap room where I could rest my foot for a few days. The hotel agreed to let me stay in my room for $48 a night, so the money that

Byron gave me would take care of two nights with a little left over! I was so grateful and reminded of Ephesians 3:20, "Now to Him who is able to do immeasurably more than all we ask or imagine, according to His power that is at work within us..." God's gifts are always more than we could ask for or even imagine!

I spent three days at the hotel, two with my foot on ice. All of this was made possible by the room Shelley had gotten for me on the first night. Of course, the meeting with her and the room were provided by the Lord Himself! He gets all the glory. And God continued to connect me with people who blessed me and whom I hopefully blessed as well.

As far as my bike, the rubber on the left floorboard had fallen off so I needed to remedy the situation before getting back on the road. I ran into a maintenance employee and asked if he possibly had a drill I could use. I was thankful that he had one which allowed me to drill a few holes in the floorboard and apply some zip ties, which would allow me to continue my journey (once my foot was well enough to ride again).

I met Abraham at the hotel and spoke with him. At that time, we noticed that a fight had broken out between a man and woman in a vehicle parked in the lot. We prayed and extended our hands out towards the car. Miraculously the couple stopped fighting, and we were able to pray with the woman.

Voodoo had contacted me and told me that her sister, Rhonda, lived in the area and wanted to meet me. On the day before I left the hotel, Rhonda invited me over to hear about my journey. I had a great time speaking with her about all that the Lord was doing. As the conversation continued, she invited me to stay for dinner with the family. She also graciously offered to put me up for the night in her home, but I already had a place to stay that evening.

The next morning, I was on my way to breakfast when I met a cleaning lady named Diana. I felt God leading me to her and I immediately saw pain in her eyes as I approached. I asked if I could pray for her and she welcomed my invitation. When I finished praying, she was crying. She believed that God led me to her that morning, giving her the encouragement that she needed.

After three nights there, my foot was feeling better and I said my goodbyes to Andrew and Byron. I am so grateful for the divine appointments which I would have missed if not for my swollen foot and the connections my Lord had orchestrated.

EVERGLADES ADVENTURES

1 Timothy 6:17 says, "Command those who are rich in this present world not to be arrogant nor to put their hope in wealth, which is so uncertain, but to put their hope in God, who richly provides us with everything for our enjoyment." The last part of that verse spoke to me throughout my journey. God had shown me so much beauty and given me so many opportunities to enjoy things I was passionate about. I am eternally grateful for all He has done!

One thing I enjoy is the hit TV show, "Gator Boys." I was headed to the Everglades and wanted to see and meet people from the show, particularly "Paul." When I arrived at the Everglades Holiday Park in Fort Lauderdale, Florida, it was getting dark. I did not see anyone from the show but talked to several people about Jesus and my journey. I left there and asked the Lord where I would stay that night. He led me up a road in Southwest Ranches, Florida, where I came upon a bright light on the right side of the road. The sign said, "Grace Baptist Church." There was a large round pavilion which would be perfect for my sleeping bag. I settled in for the night and went to sleep.

The next morning, I went to the local travel center to use the bathroom and grab breakfast. I met Jay who gave me a donation for gas and provisions. I thanked him and headed back to the church. I wanted to talk to someone from the church and let them know that I had spent the night under their pavilion. It was the right thing to do.

I noticed a car parked outside and the church doors were open, so I went inside. That's where I met Pastor Jay. I introduced myself and told the pastor that I had spent the night on church property. "I hope that was okay?" Pastor Jay responded graciously: "That's no problem at all, how long are you in town?" I told him my plans and he responded, "Stay as long as you like. We have a breaker box in the pavilion. Feel free to flip it on for lights and electricity to charge your phone. Make it your home!" Wow, once again God had amazed me beyond belief. I met a number of great people there, including Deborah, who wanted to hear more about my journey.

143

When I walked back to the parking lot, I noticed a police officer sitting nearby. I rode over to let him know that I was staying in the pavilion and that the pastor had approved it. The officer's name was Andy and he listened as I told him my story and what I was doing. He was excited about my journey and handed me a generous donation.

The next day, a friend from back home, surprised me as he pulled into the parking lot of the church. This was another "coincidence." His business had to send some parts to Florida by a certain date but the shipping company could not guarantee on-time delivery. Therefore, Mike rented a car and drove the parts to Florida himself. He had been following my journey on Facebook and saw a picture of the church so he brought his sleeping bag and joined me. We were preparing to stay under the pavilion that night but then, Deborah, the woman from the church I had talked to previously, contacted me. She and her husband secured a hotel for me for several nights so that I could attend church with them on Sunday. Mike stayed with me that evening at the hotel before he had to be on his way.

That night when Mike and I went to the hotel, he contacted someone at the U.S. Military Vets Motorcycle Club. Mike has connections and phone numbers for leaders of this club, across the country. The club member said, "I'll have 'Crash' call you." Before Mike could hang up, Crash sent him a text message, arranging for us to meet. Mike and I met Crash and a man named Erick at a local restaurant where we had a great time. Mike and I then followed Crash and Erick over to a local biker bar where I spent much of the evening talking about my journey. Jesus calls us to go into all of the world and share the Gospel, so I am always

144

willing to do just that, wherever He sends me. People who need the Lord often don't show up in our churches; we need to go where they are!

Even though Mike left the following morning, Crash sent me a message inviting me to hang out with him and members of the motorcycle club at the biker bar. I was reminded of 1 Corinthians 9 and the last part of verse 22 where the apostle Paul said, "I have become all things to all people so that by all possible means I might save some." I saw this as another divine appointment, to go where God needed me to be, so I gladly accepted the invitation.

At the bar I met a man named "Wrecker" and I spoke to him for most of the evening about Jesus and my journey. When the conversation got too deep for him, he would stop me and say, "I don't believe it, let's talk about something else." So, I would change the topic and talk about things like motorcycles. Then amazingly, he would stop me again and ask more questions about my journey. He'd say things like, "Wait, did that really happen?" It went on this way for most of the night. By "last call," at the end of the evening, Wrecker shook my hand and gave me a biker hug. What he said next really made me feel special but also confirmed that this was where God wanted me to be: "Lots of people have talked to me about Jesus but you're the first person who has really made me think about Him." Times like this reminded me of why I was on this journey.

A few days later, officer Andy showed back up at the church. He asked me if I had plans for breakfast. He wanted to hear more about my journey which, as you know by now, I was always eager to talk about! We went to a local restaurant and were talking when he received a call on his police radio. He had to rush off but handed me an additional, generous donation. I ended up with two breakfasts that morning! As I was leaving, I had the opportunity to share my story with a group of retired officers and military personnel. I am so grateful for these fine people who put their lives on the line each day for all of us.

I had a similar sentiment when I met several officers at a "Mission Barbecue" restaurant in Weston, Florida. I was able to share my story and pray with them. My emotions got the best of me there as I took in the tokens of gratitude displayed in the restaurant, and a complete appreciation for what the military and first responders do. I cried the entire time I was there! Before leaving, I thanked the manager for all that the restaurant does for those who serve us. He gave me a free dessert and some gift cards. I was so moved that I made another Facebook live video of my experience there. Check it out at
https://tinyurl.com/JR-PrayersForThoseWhoServe

Back home in Pennsylvania, before I had left on my journey, my cousin Crissy gave me some cash. She told me, "I want you to use this money for two things. First, eat a real Maine lobster for me. Second, do something you want to do." I had checked the first one off of my list early on, when I was in Maine. Now I was in the place where I could do the thing I wanted to do: experience an airboat ride through the Everglades. I had an amazing time as we traveled through these tropical wetlands. I saw a variety of wildlife, including iguanas, an alligator, and many types of birds. I had hoped to see a python or two, but never did.

Thanks to my cousin, I had experienced an awesome wonder of God's creation!

I finally had the opportunity to make my way back to Holiday Park to see if I could meet Paul from the Gator Boys show. When I arrived, there he was, finishing up a performance. I walked up to Paul and shared some of my story with him. We had a picture taken together and I was thrilled to check this item off of my dream list. It was time to leave the Everglades area and head north to see what God had planned for me next.

AMAZING ENCOUNTERS ON THE GULF COAST

As I made my way north through Florida it was time to find a place to stay for the night. I used Bunk-A-Biker as I had a number of times before. This is how I got to know "Dee," who met me for supper and treated me to a nice meal. I shared my story with her and she was amazed at what she heard. I was only looking to stay for a night when Dee asked, "How long are you in town?" I had no concrete plans, so Dee said, "If you stay with me until the end of the week, we'll go for a ride together." So that's what I did.

I rode around Dunedin, Florida and came across a crashed sailboat, with a beautiful sunset in the background. A woman was there taking pictures of the boat when she noticed me. "Pull your bike down there and I'll get a picture of you with the boat," she told me. That picture she took is probably my favorite one from the journey and what you see on the cover of this book!

The following day I rode by the same boat and sensed God telling me to pull in and take another photo. I argued because it didn't make sense; this wouldn't make a good picture, I reasoned. But that voice persisted and I wondered if He was up to something (again) beyond my imagination. So, I pulled in and tried to take a selfie, but my arm wasn't long enough to capture myself, the bike, and the boat. Now what?

A man named Ken was sitting on a nearby park bench and offered to take my picture. Rather than have him walk down to me, I said, "Can you catch?" He said "Yes," so I tossed my phone up the hill to him. He took a few pictures and I told him to toss it back down. But he said he wanted to talk to me. So, he walked down the hill, and said, "That's a nice bike, and a lot of stuff on there. What are you doing?" I told him my story, starting with what led to this journey; the fact that I was about to put a bullet in my head when God spoke so clearly to me. Ken was wearing sunglasses but I could see tears when I got to that part of the story. I asked, "Are you okay, brother?" Through his tears he said, "No, I'm not. I was sitting on that bench deciding how I was going to kill myself tomorrow. I heard your bike coming and God spoke to me and said that He was sending me an angel on a Harley. Then you came and I heard your story. It gives me hope."

We cried together and hugged. Only God could create moments like this. We exchanged numbers and I texted him every day for a while, and we still keep in touch to this day. In one of his messages Ken told me, "If you wouldn't have stopped that day, I wouldn't be here. You saved my life that day and you didn't even know it." All I

148

could do was give glory to God. This was His journey and He orchestrated these divine appointments as only He can do.

During the week when I stayed with Dee, I would typically ride around and tell people about Jesus. I had heard about "Hogan's Hangout," the restaurant of retired professional wrestler/tv personality, Hulk Hogan, so I headed to Clearwater to see it. Of course, I wanted to continue telling people my story, but I also wanted to meet Mr. Hogan.

I visited Hogan's Hangout as well as "Hogan's Beach Shop" a few doors down. A friend from back home was following me on Facebook and had sent me Hulk's address. So, I thought I would go there and see if I could meet him. I also wanted to arm wrestle him! (I know it sounds crazy but I thought it would be a fun thing to do!) I could only get as far as his driveway so I revved up my bike a few times, hoping he might hear it and come out to meet me. But it wasn't to be. Maybe on another journey?

On Saturday of that week, I went for the ride with Dee. We had a great time seeing the sights in the area, including a building constructed out of old movie tins. On Sunday we went to the "Salvation Saloon," a church which meets in a bar. The bar is closed on Sundays when church services are held. The pastor is an ex-police officer who followed God's call into ministry. Amazingly, he knew some of the same guys I got to know from the Biker Church USA Church of Maine, my first stop of the journey! After a great service and time of worship, the pastor gave me a donation to continue my journey.

149

Spur called and told me about a connection he had in Massachusetts. A man named Jeff knew a guy in Florida who was associated with "Celebrate Recovery" (CR), a Christ-centered, recovery program for anyone struggling with hurt, pain or addiction of any kind. Spur asked me to call Jeff who then asked me to call a man named "Luckey." I contacted Luckey and shared my story with him. He then invited me to New Walk Church for a CR meeting that evening. I asked Luckey about places to stay in the area and he agreed to let me know. So, I headed to Zephyrhills, which is northeast of Tampa.

When I arrived at the church, I was greeted by Luckey, Ty, and Danny. Ty introduced himself and said, "You're staying with my wife Theresa and I tonight so don't worry about anything." I still smile when I think about this and all of the times God provided for me on this journey! I had a great time at the CR meeting, listening to the stories and talking to a few people afterwards.

I told Ty that my bike had been making a noise. Ty took me to see a man called, "The Dave," who agreed to try and fix my bike. The plan was to drop my bike off on Sunday. The Dave was so moved when I told him about my journey, he agreed to donate his labor, and that I would just need to raise money for the parts. I shared my need on Facebook and got exactly what I needed to cover the bill for the parts. All praise to God!

I met so many nice people during my time here. I met a 13-year-old girl named Kylie who has amazing faith and a powerful passion to serve God. Kylie is involved with a number of ministries at New Walk Church and she really blessed my heart. After I shared my story with her, she removed her WWJD bracelet and placed it on my wrist. I wear it to this day, reminding me of this wonderful young girl and how God is using her for His Kingdom.

It was now February, and I would be spending my birthday in Florida. I dropped off my bike and Luckey and his wife Margie took me out to dinner for my birthday. I was so humbled and grateful for this wonderful gesture. While at the restaurant I spoke with a man named Josh and his family about my journey. I learned that they had a dream of buying a bus, homeschooling their children, and traveling around the country to share the Gospel. This encounter evidently gave them the "push" they needed to follow their dream and God's plan for their lives. They purchased a bus and converted it to a motorhome. In October of 2021, just before I wrote this book, I received a message from Josh: he was coming through Pennsylvania and wanted to visit me. We met at a local restaurant where they graciously treated me to lunch. When we left the restaurant, I took their two boys for rides around the parking lot. I then led them around the area, showing the family the sights and the beauty God created where I live. Their oldest son rode on my bike with me, which was an adventure for him. I am so blessed at how I had met this family only twice and they placed such trust in me. Only God can make these kinds of connections. His ways are so much higher than anything I could come up with or imagine!

AN UNEXPECTED DETOUR

Jesus said in John 16:33, "I have told you these things, so that in Me you may have peace. In this world you will have trouble. But take heart! I have overcome the world." Those words became especially meaningful for me during my time in the Zephyrhills/Tampa area.

My bike was at the shop and I was staying with Ty and Theresa. On this particular day, I was walking around the house and felt severe pains in my groin area. When I would lie down, the pain would subside. Ty and Theresa were headed to the local Walmart for a few items and asked if I wanted to come along. I agreed to go, but things went downhill quickly as I walked around the store. I was in excruciating pain. The severe pain suddenly quit, then a slight pain went down my right leg, then up my right side. Based on what was happening, I was pretty certain that my IVC (Inferior Vena Cava) filter had become dislodged.

Doctors had implanted the IVC filter in my groin back in 2005 after a car accident. I had a history of blood clots and the filter would prevent a catastrophic event such as a pulmonary embolism. The filter was supposed to stay in place for life but I could feel it travelling through my body. I felt sick to my stomach and was ready to pass out. I told Theresa that something was wrong.

As predicted, I passed out and hit the floor. Shortly thereafter I came to and tried to get up, but I went down again. Finally, I sat up against a freezer unit and someone called an ambulance. Looking back, I am so grateful that I wasn't on my bike when this occurred. Once again, God held me in the palm of His hand.

When I arrived at the hospital, I was first tested for COVID. Surprisingly I tested positive. Doctors performed a heart catheterization procedure but everything looked good. I told them about my IVC filter which led to a chest x-ray. The x-ray revealed that the IVC filter had become dislodged and was now stuck in my heart. Thankfully, I had not suffered a heart attack, but my situation was still serious; the filter had to come out.

I was transported to a hospital in Tampa where I spent the next 24 days. I was isolated for 10 days due to COVID, then surgery was delayed a week. Additionally, the surgeon was on vacation which extended the delay. Time flies when you're having fun! (Not really!) But God was still working and had a purpose and complete control of the timing.

At times I would ask God, "Why am I in here for so long?" His response was, "Because people need to hear about Jesus." And that statement was confirmed; I talked to so many people during my stay. I would typically ask everyone I encountered: "Do you know Jesus, do you have a personal relationship with Him, and are you going to heaven?" There were many great conversations. Many people claim to know Jesus but lack the assurance that He wants us to have. 1 John 5:13 gives us this promise: "I write these things to you who believe in the name of the Son of God, that you may know that you have eternal life."

What a blessing it was to experience hospital-led prayer each morning and evening. At 8 a.m. each day, a prayer was shared over the loudspeaker. At 8 p.m. each evening, the hospital closed the day with prayer. The nurses and staff were amazing, too! I got to know many of them well and there were many opportunities for me to share Jesus with the staff.

During my stay in the hospital, my bike had been fixed. Ty and Theresa took it back to their home for safe-keeping. They took care of my personal items and kept in touch with me while I was in the hospital. Ty and Luckey also visited me. I was blessed when Ty told me that I would stay at his house until I was healed and well enough to travel again. I am so grateful for these friends God brought into my life.

When it was finally time for surgery, the procedure only took about one hour and it thankfully went very well. The doctor went into a vein in my neck/chest area to retrieve the filter from my heart. I learned that the doctor who ultimately performed the surgery had also traveled to Haiti on missions trips. I was blessed to know this since I have taken similar trips and have such a passion for the people there, especially the children.

I stayed with Ty and Theresa a few more weeks. After the surgery and long stay in the hospital, I could hardly walk due to sciatica pain. It was early March before I felt well enough to get back on the road.

I left Ty and Theresa's early one morning to head to Inglis, Florida. I learned that Lil Wolf would be speaking at the Scooter Haven Country Club, a campground for bikers. I wanted to go and support him for all he'd done for me on my journey. This one-and-a-half-hour drive would be the longest ride I had taken since being released from the hospital. I praise God that I made the trip without incident!

I arrived at the club before Lil Wolf. When he showed up, we greeted each other and had breakfast together. It was so nice to catch up with my friend and brother! Lil Wolf walked away for a few minutes and then came back. He said to me, "When I'm done talking, I want you to share your journey with the people." What a blessing from my friend! I had come to listen to him, but then had the opportunity to share my story with lots of people! I then received a generous donation for my ministry, thanks to Lil Wolf, the club, and some of the campers who were there. After a great time there I rode back to Ty and Theresa's place to spend the night.

DAYTONA

Ty and some guys from the club decided to ride to Daytona Bike Week, and I was invited to go along. We stopped at Rick's Café for a bite to eat. As we prepared to pay the bill, the waitress surprised us and said that everything had been taken care of. There were at least six of us there so the bill wasn't cheap. Evidently a guy in the restaurant saw our group and decided to "pay it forward." He showed his gratitude because some bikers had recently stopped to help him.

We arrived at the Daytona International Speedway and checked out the vendors on site. We rode around Daytona for a while and then headed back to Zephyrhills together. The very next day I returned to Daytona to hang out with the Hellfighters from Pensacola. They had invited me to come back and spend time with them. They would provide all accommodations, all I had to do was get myself there. So, after spending the night at Ty and Theresa's, I turned right around and headed back to Daytona.

I had a feeling that Dee might be in town so I sent her a message. Sure enough, she was in town, so we met up and enjoyed walking around, visiting vendors at the Speedway. The divine appointments continued as I recognized my new friend from Oatman, Arizona: Grizzly! I was so blessed that he remembered me! We all had a wonderful time together. God had amazed me once again!

I stayed in a condo with the Hellfighters on a mission that was part telling people about Jesus and part enjoying fellowship with them. They fed me, bought my gas, and took complete care of me! I am so grateful for all they did for me!

While I was in Daytona, Tiny called and invited me to the Outlaw's clubhouse. Tiny and a group of Outlaws were in Daytona while I was there! So, I hung out with Outlaws from all over the United States. There were pop-up canopies with food and items for sale, along with a live band. It was also a blessing to see Lil Wolf, Voodoo, and Hoss while I was there!

That night, Tiny and I slept outdoors, outside the Outlaw's clubhouse fence. The weather was nice and I always enjoyed sleeping under the stars when the temperature was warm enough. The next day, I joined Lil Wolf, Hoss, his wife Voodoo, the Hellfighters, and some other great people at a local church where we handed out food to the less fortunate. I made some great connections there and was grateful to see how different clubs and people were working together for a common cause. In a real way, I was seeing Jesus's prayer in John 17:21 being answered in real-time, "that all of them may be one, Father, just as You are in Me and I am in You. May they also be in Us so that the world may believe that You have sent Me."

BLESSINGS IN INGLIS

The next day I rode to a nearby campground in Inglis, Florida. Rodney and Cindee, Jason's parents, were vacationing there and had been following my journey on social media. They sent me a message, inviting me to stop by and see them if I was in the area. The timing was perfect and we enjoyed a great time of fellowship and "catching up" at their campsite. And I finally got the opportunity to touch a snake! I heard Cindee scream as she came upon a black snake. I was able to catch the little fella and relocate him up the road, far away from Cindee! Did I mention that I love snakes?

Two other friends from home, Jim and Karen, were vacationing in the area with Rodney and Cindee. What a blessing it was to spend time with them as well! My four friends took me out and treated me to a wonderful supper.

157

I just "happened" to be right near Scooter Haven Country Club and that is where I spent the night. The folks there were amazing as they gave me an open invitation to stay there anytime. They did everything for me and provided for all of my needs. I am so thankful to the Lord and these folks for all they did! The next morning, I had breakfast with Rodney, Cindee, Jim, and Karen, who graciously took care of the bill. It was such a blessing to spend time with them and confirmation of yet another divine appointment.

After breakfast, I headed back to Ty and Theresa's place. We went to the New Walk Church and met up with Pastor Eddy, Paul, and Jeff. After hearing my story, Paul and Jeff gave me a very generous donation to keep my ministry going.

After that, I went to Danny's house where he showed me some really cool "guy" stuff; he had several bikes and all kinds of memorabilia. His collection reminded me of my grandparents' house when I was a boy and it brought back wonderful memories!

I stayed in the area for a few more days. When it was time to leave, Ty, Theresa, Luckey, Danny, Adam and his son, Pastor Eddy, Ken, and Roy treated me to a wonderful farewell breakfast. As usual the Lord had a few divine appointments lined up and I talked to our server and a couple about my journey.

Looking back, I had stayed on and off with Ty and Theresa for the better part of a month. I can't overstate how very appreciative I am that this couple took in a man they did not know and did so much for me. For a couple to open up their house, provide for all of my needs, and trust me even when they were away from home, is just not something you see every day in our society. They were truly the hands and feet of Jesus. Of course, there are so many others who helped me and went above and beyond the call. I love and am so grateful for my new family across this great country!

It was finally time to go so I left breakfast and made a beeline back to Pensacola.

Dee, Grizzly and I

My fourth corner: Key West, Florida.
Christmas Day 2020

THE FINAL STOP

Tiny had called me while I was in the hospital and said that he wanted me to stop by his place before I headed back home to Pennsylvania. He said (jokingly, of course), that he would come up to Pennsylvania and give me a good whooping if I didn't stop by and see him. I replied (tongue-in-cheek, of course) that I might just go back to Pennsylvania and see if he would actually come and do it! To be sure, Tiny had become a great friend and there was no way I was going home without stopping by to spend time with him. We hit it off immediately when we first met and developed a special connection. I love my brother!

Back at Tiny's house, I was fascinated on a regular basis by the Blue Angels. The team is stationed at the Naval Air Station in Pensacola during the air show season. They conduct precision flight demonstrations which showcase the professionalism and teamwork found in the Navy and Marine Corps. They also perform a great deal of community service in each air show city across the country. Due to their proximity to Tiny's house, the Blue Angels would fly directly overhead as they trained. I was in awe of not only the roaring sound of the aircraft but also the precision, speed, and beauty of their formations.

I was blessed to spend time with Tiny, doing a few odd jobs and helping him with house and yard work. The physical activity did take its toll and I was reminded of the health issues I had which led up to my journey. I was in pain for a few days after the repeated bending and strenuous movements but I cherish the time Tiny and I spent together.

On Easter Sunday morning I had one of the most powerful "mountaintop" experiences with the Lord, ever! Tiny invited me to accompany him and his son to the sunrise service at Blue Wahoos Stadium. The beauty of the sunrise reminded me of the most awesome "Son-rise;" the resurrection of my Lord and Savior, Jesus Christ. I get emotional even as I write this, thinking about the beauty of that sunrise, the praise and worship, and the message at the service. I am not good with numbers but estimate that there were thousands of people packed into the stadium for this amazing time of worship. I can't describe the feeling; it's something I will never forget.

All told, I spent the better part of three weeks with Tiny. Of course, everywhere I went; for meals, to clubs, to the barber shop, I talked with everyone about Jesus. That's the reason I believe God had me on this journey.

Guys from the Living Room clubhouse held a "going-away" party for me just before I planned to leave Pensacola. I was so blessed by the abundant food, music, and fellowship. These brothers also blessed me with another generous donation for my ministry before I left.

After the wonderful party at the Living Room, I went back to Tiny's house and packed up my belongings. Tiny and his son Dylan had already left for Alabama so that Dylan could race at the motocross event. My plan was to join Tiny at the race and then head home to Pennsylvania. I left Tiny's place at about 1 a.m. and rode to Alabama. When I arrived, I met Tiny and Dylan at their hotel. There were still a few hours before the race so Tiny graciously allowed me to get a couple hours of sleep in his hotel room.

I was so privileged to be there with Tiny and to see his son Dylan race. I believe that Dylan is about thirteen years old and he is quite the dirt bike racer. I thoroughly enjoyed our time together and said my farewell to my brother and his son. I left at about 1 in the afternoon and finally pointed my bike towards home.

HOMEWARD BOUND

The only reason I left Florida and ended my journey when I did, was to attend a wedding back home. Jason's wife BJ waited 10 years and two days from his death to remarry. She wanted me to be at the wedding and there was no way I was going to miss it.

I rode until about 8:30 that night and made it to the Virginia/West Virginia border It was dark and I saw deer everywhere. You probably can imagine that deer and motorcycles don't mix very well! I was grateful to find a hotel where I could get some rest and then finish my ride home safely in the morning. As usual the Lord had a divine appointment for me at the hotel. I shared my story with the clerk at the front desk. She was moved by what I was doing and gave me the "Soldier's Discount." She told me, "You are a soldier for Jesus!" God had provided for me yet again, as He had so abundantly on my journey. After a great sleep I woke up early and rode in the rain to Pennsylvania.

When I crossed the state line between Maryland and Pennsylvania, I took note of the sign which said: "Welcome to Pennsylvania. Pursue Your Happiness." I thought about that slogan and realized that this is exactly what God had allowed me to do on this epic journey. While He had given me a mission, He also gave me the opportunity to pursue my happiness. Riding my Harley and telling people about Jesus are two things that make me happy!

Before arriving at my house, I stopped at my favorite store in the area. The employees at the local Rutter's know me well and were happy to see me after my long absence. I grabbed a coffee and ordered what is well-known to the employees as a "Jimmy Wrap." The Jimmy Wrap is a cheesy hashbrown wrap which employees named after me due to my frequent visits to the store. They all know how to make a Jimmy Wrap when I come into the store and they all have fun with it. I never know exactly what it will look like because I allow them to put whatever they want on it. Sometimes they actually "fight" over who gets to make the wrap! It was so good to be back home!

At about noon on April 12, 2021, I arrived at my house. I rested for a bit before my daughter Heavyn stopped by with her little brother and sister. The four of us sat down and caught up. It was an awesome blessing to hug and kiss my daughter, and tell her that I love her, after being away for so long. I continue to pray every day for her and I know that others do as well. The Bible says in Luke 18:1, "Then Jesus told his disciples a parable to show them that they should always pray and not give up." He has a plan for Heavyn's life, as He does for all of us, so I will never stop praying for her.

166

I had been on the road for six months and two days, accumulating a total of 20,464 miles on my Harley. Amazingly, I came home with more gifts, resources, and money than I had when I left. God had been faithful and so good to me every moment of the journey, just as He had promised. Now I wondered what He was going to do next.

THE JOURNEY CONTINUES

I had only been home for two days when depression set in. I was miserable and didn't quite understand why after all that had happened. I cried out to God, "How can I be depressed when You just gave me the journey of a lifetime?" I sensed God telling me, "It's because you're not done yet, son. Get out there and continue telling people about me." So, the day after BJ's wedding, I was back on my bike and I hit the road. I spent three weeks in the Taunton, Massachusetts area, catching up with friends and telling people about Jesus. Then I returned home for two more weddings.

After that short second journey, I stayed home for about five weeks. I asked the Lord, "What do You want me to do next? As long as You provide, I will ride." I attended another wedding where a friend handed me some money which I placed in my pocket. When I got home, I discovered that the donation was extremely generous. Then other donations came to me. My friend Kyle, who I met back in

Bangor at the beginning of my journey, invited me back for 4th of July weekend. I sensed God nudging me to go so I did. I rode to Bangor and then to the very top of Maine at the Canadian border.

Remember Dee and Gail who had blessed me on my journey when I was in Florida? I had met Dee through Bunk-A-Biker and spent several days with her. I met Gail on a beach and learned that she had a ministry like mine, except that she rides around in her car. Now while I was back in Maine, God was once again orchestrating a divine appointment down in Florida. Dee sent me a text message which read something like this: "Billboard, you amaze me. I am standing in line at a rally and I met your friend, Gail." Dee included a picture of herself and Gail in the text!

I was blown away! Dee and Gail were from the same general area in Florida but had never met. Evidently, they were standing in line, at a very large rally, and exchanged small talk. Gail spoke to Dee about Jesus and happened to mention a man she had met on the beach, and has a similar ministry to hers except that he rides a motorcycle. Dee replied that she had met a friend in Florida who rides a Harley, telling people about Jesus. When they put two and two together, they realized that they were talking about the same person! What are the chances? I've learned that when God is involved, anything is possible!

I returned to Taunton and a woman contacted me on social media, asking if I was going to Sturgis for bike week. I responded that God didn't tell me to go and I couldn't afford it anyway. I said, "If God wants me to go, He will make a way." Within a week I had received about $1200

170

in donations and sensed God telling me to go to Sturgis and tell people about Jesus. My childhood dream had been realized at last!

As I talk to people about my journey, many bikers have told me that I am living their dream. And I freely admit that God granted me this dream ministry and it's been wonderful. God is using my story to tell others about Him. I have thoroughly enjoyed reliving this journey by writing about it, and I don't believe this will be the last book. I know that God has more for me to do and it's just a matter of time before I hit the road again. My journey will continue.

As long as He provides, I will ride.

YOUR OWN JOURNEY:
A FINAL WORD

The book you hold in your hand describes just a portion of the many, many blessings I experienced along the way. But in spite of the joy and wonderful experiences, it wasn't easy.

There were times when I was cold, wet, hungry, in dangerous conditions, in ill health, and discouraged. I often didn't know where food, gas, and shelter would come from. But God provided in every situation. The trials and troubles came, but He walked through every one of them with me. He used miracles and many people to bless me and others.

Proverbs 3:5 – 6 says, "Trust in the Lord with all your heart and lean not on your own understanding; in all your ways submit to Him, and He will make your paths straight." Through my journey I discovered first hand that this Scripture is true. When our eyes are on Jesus and we trust in His wisdom, not our own, He makes the way straight.

My friend, I believe that this life is a lot like my journey. There are blessings and times of great joy, but there are also trials. Jesus told us that there would be trouble as long as we live on this earth. But having Him and His Word to guide us, we can trust God to get us through those tough times.

Whether you realize it or not, you and I are on a journey to a destination. Remember my ride through the "Tunnel of Trees?" It reminded me of Matthew 7:13 - 14 which bears repeating. Jesus said, "Enter through the narrow gate. For wide is the gate and broad is the road that leads to destruction, and many enter through it. But small is the gate and narrow the road that leads to life, and only a few find it." Which road are you on? Where will your journey lead you?

The Bible says that there is one of two places where we will spend eternity: Heaven, in the presence of God. Or hell, where people will spend forever separated from God. And there is not a thing we can do to get to heaven on our own. Romans 3:23 says, "for all have sinned and fall short of the glory of God." Romans 6:23 begins this way: "For the wages of sin is death..." You see, apart from Jesus Christ, we are all on that broad road which leads to destruction, eternal separation from God. We could never do enough good deeds to please God or work our way to heaven. My visit to the Grand Canyon reminded me of the wide chasm there is between sinful man and a Holy God. Isaiah 64:6 tells us, "All of us have become like one who is unclean, and all our righteous acts are like filthy rags; we all shrivel up like a leaf, and like the wind our sins sweep us away."

Here is the wonderful news and it's stated in the continuation of Romans 6:23: "... but the gift of God is eternal life in Christ Jesus our Lord." God gave us this gift through the death, burial, and resurrection of Jesus Christ. Jesus paid the price we could never pay by shedding His blood on a cruel cross. He took on the sins of the whole world, including your sins and mine. His resurrection from the dead gives us the certainty that we too will be resurrected. But we need to make a decision to receive this gift, just as I did in that little Pennsylvania country church.

Romans 10:9 clearly states, "If you declare with your mouth, 'Jesus is Lord,' and believe in your heart that God raised Him from the dead, you will be saved." The Bible is clear that we need a Savior, we must be adopted into God's family to be on that narrow road. John 1:12 says, "Yet to all who did receive Him, to those who believed in His name, He gave the right to become children of God."

Have you made the decision to give your heart and life to Jesus? Is your journey taking you to heaven? The days are short and none of us is guaranteed tomorrow. James 4:14 says, "Why, you do not even know what will happen tomorrow. What is your life? You are a mist that appears for a little while and then vanishes." There is an urgency to get right with God right now. Hebrews 3:15 says, "As has just been said: "Today, if you hear His voice, do not harden your hearts as you did in the rebellion."

There will come a day, very soon, when we will face the Lord, either to spend a glorious eternity with Him or to be condemned forever to hell. Hebrews 9:27-28 tells us, "Just as people are destined to die once, and after that to face judgment, so Christ was sacrificed once to take away the sins of many; and He will appear a second time, not to bear sin, but to bring salvation to those who are waiting for Him." Are you waiting for Him?

In the Introduction I said, "Know that our souls will live for eternity in one of two places: heaven or hell. Choose wisely my friends." That is my prayer for everyone I meet and each one that picks up this book. I don't want to see anyone make the devastating choice to stay on the broad road.

If you haven't already, won't you give your life to Jesus right now? Romans 10:9, which I shared above, states things so clearly. Just pray a simple prayer, in your own words, but with a sincere heart. Tell the Lord that you recognize that you are a sinner, in thought, word, and actions. Confess and turn from your sins, asking Him to forgive you by the blood of Jesus Christ. Receive Him as Lord and Savior, and vow to live for Him, with the help of His Holy Spirit, to lead and guide you on your journey.

If you are sincere about this decision, it is life-changing. You won't be perfect and you won't live a problem-free life, but you'll have joy, peace, and purpose you never had before. And it is a journey unlike anything you can imagine!

2 Corinthians 5:17 confirms the great transformation your life will experience when you receive Jesus Christ as Lord and Savior: "Therefore, if anyone is in Christ, the new creation has come: The old has gone, the new is here!"

A FINAL WORD FROM JIMMY

My friends, I come back to where I started. Jesus Christ totally transformed my life, from a sinner who ran from Him to an undeserving child of God. Without His love, patience, grace, mercy, and forgiveness, I would not be here.

The incredible journey God allowed me to take was only possible because He provided everything, through miracles, people, and that still small voice that guides me. I had so many divine appointments, holy interruptions, and "coincidences" on my journey which would fill several books. I also had the opportunity to experience the beauty of His creation and enjoy a number of adventures He made possible. I cannot express my gratitude enough to God and everyone who supported me in any way.

And remember the tent from earlier? The one I packed on my bike and never used. I might have left you wondering why. First, I assumed I would need a tent because I couldn't have imagined that God would provide a place to stay every single night of my journey. Lastly, and most significantly, after I got home, I asked God why He asked me to pack the tent. I heard Him say, "Because you needed a backrest, son." And the way it was packed, that tent was part of the backrest on my bike. You see, once again, God knew exactly what I would need. I continue to be amazed at all He does!

If you get nothing else from this book, I humbly ask you to remember two things: First, keep your eyes fixed on Jesus and trust Him. He will never, ever let you down. Second, and related to the first point, you cannot look at my journey and not see the hand of the Lord in it. There were too many "coincidences" and miracles. He is interested in every detail of your life and will guide you on your journey, like He did for me, if you'll just allow Him to do so.

I know one thing for sure: In spite of my imperfections and flaws, God is not finished with me yet on my journey. He is still writing my story. And I know that He is not finished with you either. Jeremiah 33:3 says, "Call to Me and I will answer you and tell you great and unsearchable things you do not know."

Call to Him, trust Him, and I guarantee you that you will experience many divine encounters on your own epic quest for Jesus!

Thank you so much for reading! Hope to see you on a future journey. Until then, may God richly bless you!

Your friend,
Jimmy (a.k.a. "Billboard")

...being confident of this, that He who began a good work in you will carry it on to completion until the day of Christ Jesus.
Philippians 1:6

ABOUT THE AUTHOR: JAMES "BILLBOARD" RICE

An unlikely servant, James "Billboard" Rice found God along a rebellious road. Originally from Fort Loudon, Pennsylvania, Jimmy loves riding his Harley and telling people about Jesus and what He's done in his own life. With quite a checkered road behind him, he is amazed that God has forgiven him and has since taken on the mission to go make disciples and lead others to Jesus through his testimony and love for the open road.

Besides riding his Harley, he enjoys hunting, fishing and anything else outdoors where he can take in God's awesome creation in nature. Self-proclaimed as "far from perfect," Jimmy relies solely on God to lead him through this life until called home. His love for God and others helps to keep him focused on his purpose in life, which he believes is for each of us to know our Creator and make Him known to the world! Jimmy is also father to Heavyn, his daughter, whom he adores.

Connect with Jimmy on
Facebook @james.rice.988373
or email jtr75@yahoo.com

Learn more about Epic Quest for Jesus Motorcycle Ministries at
www.epicquest4jesus.com

ABOUT ROBERT JONES

Robert Jones is an average guy from New Jersey who is also the author of *Average Man, Almighty Companion*, and *Family Love Letters*. A friend of Jimmy's, Bob felt the incredible call from God to use his talent to help write Jimmy's story. He is passionate about sharing the love of Jesus Christ with everyone he meets, through encouraging and often humorous stories. Bob is the father of three amazing grown daughters and lives in Central Pennsylvania with his

wife of 36+ years. He enjoys music, hiking, reading, and of course, writing books and blogs.

Connect with Bob online through his website AverageManMessage.com.

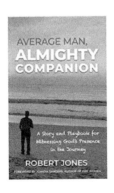

Bob's other publications are also available on Amazon and BarnesandNoble.com

ABOUT JOANNA SANDERS

A new friend of Jimmy's, Joanna was instantly moved to want to be involved in helping Jimmy tell his story to the world. Joanna is a graduate of Villanova University and Moody Theological Seminary. She's the founder and head writer of Colossians46.com, which provides biblical content support, writing, and editing. She loves helping other authors realize God's purpose through their stories and reflecting His glory back through their words. Joanna has written for several Christian publications and has a heart for women's ministry. Joanna is the author of *Fire Women: Sexual Purity & Submission for the Passionate Woman* and co-author of *Disciple Trip* with Dr. Joey Cook. Most importantly, she is wife to Geoff and mom to three godly-men-in-training.

Connect with Joanna at Colossians46.com

ABOUT THE MINISTRY

Epic Quest for Jesus Motorcycle Ministries was founded by James "Billboard" Rice after the incredible epic quest of riding his Harley 20,464 miles around the four corners of the United States to tell people about Jesus. Realizing that the ride is far from over, Jimmy continues to commit that "if God provides, he will ride" wherever God leads him to continue to share the Gospel and make disciples. Knowing that sometimes the "ride" doesn't need to go much further than our own neighborhood, EQFJ Ministries is devoted to showing the hope of Christ, love, acceptance, and strength for anyone in need. As the ministry expands, Jimmy plans to have efforts specifically devoted to helping the homeless in this country, as well as the youth—the next generation.

To learn more, or support the ministry, please visit
www.epicquest4jesus.com

ADDITIONAL COPIES OF THIS BOOK
MAY BE PURCHASED ON
AMAZON.COM
OR BARNESANDNOBLE.COM

Made in the USA
Middletown, DE
23 September 2022

11054925R00116